Psychology for
Successful Evangelism

Psychology for Successful Evangelism

By
JAMES H. JAUNCEY

Foreword by
LEIGHTON FORD

MOODY PRESS • Chicago

© 1972 by
THE MOODY BIBLE INSTITUTE
OF CHICAGO

Library of Congress Catalog Card Number: 75-175499

ISBN: 0-8024-6940-X

Printed in the United States of America

CONTENTS

CHAPTER		PAGE
	Foreword	7
	Preface	9
1.	Psychology and God's Purposes	11
2.	Psychology and Evangelism	17
3.	The Individual Beyond His Own Skin	23
4.	The Basic Drive	33
5.	Cause Hunger	45
6.	The Drive to Belong	55
7.	Identification	66
8.	Rapport	74
9.	Background Rapport	83
10.	The Power of Guilt	91
11.	The Power of Suggestion	99
12.	Experimental Results	105
13.	Mass Media	116
14.	The Personal Angle	122

FOREWORD

DR. JAUNCEY has done an admirable job of showing how man's basic psychological drives are met in the gospel. He writes lucidly, with theological insight and psychological balance. This book helps us to see how man's psychological makeup must be taken into account in effective sharing of our faith. Yet he gives full place to the work of the Spirit of God and the dignity of human nature. Dr. Jauncey is committed passionately to the gospel, yet not afraid to criticize where necessary some of our methods of evangelism. I heartily commend this book to pastors, evangelists, and laymen alike.

LEIGHTON FORD

PREFACE

THIS IS NOT a book on techniques of evangelism. Its purpose is much more basic. It seeks to describe those drives which motivate human response, especially to the message of the gospel. It is directed to the ordinary minister, and does not assume any psychological training on his part. My conviction is that once these principles are understood, the pastor, knowing the people in his community, will have the skill to apply them with satisfying effect. My hope is that evangelism will be made more effective by replacing guesswork and hit-and-miss methods with a Spirit-directed scientific approach.

No attempt has been made to produce a comprehensive academic text. The design is practical. I have confined myself to those factors which I have found to be especially relevant to the task of the evangelist. There is nothing here that is mere theory. It has all been tested in the workshop of actual evangelistic effort.

1
PSYCHOLOGY AND GOD'S PURPOSES

AT FIRST GLANCE, bringing psychology in to to help with evangelism seems like bringing in a man with his bare hands to do the job of a bulldozer. Since God is the source of all power, it would appear that He could accomplish His purposes without our puny aid. The use of psychology, therefore, looks like an admission that we do not believe the power is there, so we have to do the best we can.

But this is shallow and unobservant reasoning. The Christian farmer recognizes that everything comes from God; nevertheless, he eagerly takes advantage of the results of agricultural science. He does not place himself over against God, but rather in partnership with Him. Can we expect the sowing of the seed of the Word to be any different?

To some, conversion is just a human process of reorientation; consequently, they have to fall back on psychology in the belief that this is all they have. This is not the position of this book. After almost forty years as a Christian I am very much aware that what has been happening in me means more to me than a mere hypothesis to explain the world. I am in continuous confrontation with Him and I *know*. When I think of evangelism, therefore, I am concerned with far more than personal information. The goal is the entry of the Holy Spirit into the life to bring about a change within.

This is in no sense a denial of human processes. I am very much aware that, even in my religious experience, my emotions, attitudes, motivations, guilt feelings, drives, etc., are quite like those of a non-Christian. The orientation and the impact may be different but the elements are the same.

Neither is there any unique foreign element present. An analyst, in exploring my psyche, would not find a secret ingredient x which he would have to admit was placed there by God. He would find patterns of personality that would distinguish me from a nonreligious person, but he would not find anything that was not explainable in human terms.

Yet my consciousness of God's presence and action is not diminished in the slightest by this admission. For God is working *through* these processes, not outside them.

There is nothing unique in the elements of one's religious experience. The uniqueness comes in its configuration, its motivation, and on the grounds of its existence.

It is something like the physical world. The basic atomic structure of a tree and a dog are the same: electrons, protons, neutrons, etc., but the arrangement makes all the difference. Some of the genetic driving forces are quite different, yet an analysis would reveal the same basic building blocks.

Feelings generated by the action of God in the life may not differ in kind from any other feelings. Paul has to warn his converts not to be drunken with wine, but to be filled with the Spirit. Apparently the exuberance resulting from each was similar.

This means that God does not have to create special psychological elements in a man's personality to express religious experience. If He did, this would indicate that He erred initially in not making adequate provisions for it in human nature. God does not make that kind of mistake. The human psyche is perfectly constructed for everything that God has in mind. When He enters the heart at conversion, all the psychological machinery is there ready for His every expression.

It is important, therefore, to disabuse ourselves that there is any magic or abracadabra about conversion. It is miraculous rather than magical in that the origin of the event is supernatural, but its operation is not contrary to reason.

As Robert Thouless has put it, the psychology of religion explains conversion but does not explain it away. There is a world of difference. He says it is something like beckoning with your finger. You may scientifically explain every aspect of the act—its physics, its chemistry, its biology, and so on to exhaustion—but this does not affect the original ground of that event which was an act of your will. Similarly, you can describe the psychological processes in conversion, but it is still an act of God's will.

Psychology can never enter into the question of whether or not God is the origin or ground of religious experience; it can only study the experience. But since God is using human psychological experience, its analysis and study become extremely valuable. It is, therefore, a bad mistake to set God off over against psychology. It is not God versus psychology but God working in it and through it.

So psychology is not like a man trying to do the job of the bulldozer. It is more like a man putting the bulldozer (the power of God) into action to bring about man's response. The analogy does not imply that God is going to bulldoze the human will. Man made in the image of God cannot have his freedom infringed on in this way. His response must be willing and eager. Psychology helps to present the gospel in a way that makes this more likely.

Since this is not a book on theology, it is important at this point to not be sidetracked into the controversy regarding the relation between predestination and free will in conversion. Both election and human response are strongly emphasized in the Scriptures. But this text deals with the *practical* task of winning men—a task where there is no real difference between the Calvinist and the Arminian presentation to the unbeliever. Both seek to elicit a favorable response and both try to present their message in such a way as to provoke that reaction. Psychology is used in either case.

There is no need to justify the use of psychology in evangelism, because Christ Himself used it. Dr. H. L. Fowler, former professor of psychology at the University of Western Australia, said that the more he read the New Testament, the more he was convinced that Jesus was the greatest practicing psychologist who ever lived. He was referring to the skill in which the Lord dealt with men, and the genius with which He brought His listeners into identification with the characters in His parables.

Thus far I have been treating the term *psychology* as being almost synonymous with psychological (including religious) experience. This could lead to the overquick optimism that we have already evaluated human experience, and now all we need to do is to put the laws gained into operation and, almost automatically, win the world for Christ.

Of course, the situation is far from being this ideal. We don't possess that type of knowledge and, even if we did, the psychological determinants of an individual's behavior are so complex and unique that making an appraisal of him as a basis of approach would still be enormously difficult. But further, even if some supercomputer could produce such an evaluation, we still could not predict his response. A man's will makes him like a god, sovereign in his decisions, regardless of the contributing factors.

Psychology has many definitions. Perhaps the best here is "the science of behavior," including internal behavior (experience or consciousness) as well as external acts.

Although psychology is now a highly rigorous experimental science, it formerly was little more than generalized observation in which guesses were made as to the laws of human behavior. Today, no theory is accepted until it is thoroughly tested. Consequently, a large body of highly reliable knowledge has resulted.

Unfortunately, one of the least definitive areas is that of the personality, which has proved tantalizingly elusive to scientific analysis. However, although exact knowledge may not be greatly detailed, the broad issues are clearly known, and it is with these that we are mainly concerned.

In any case, it cannot be too strongly stressed that psychological laws are reliable only on the average and, therefore, may not apply in any particular case. In this, psychology is different from physics (except for some atomic physics) where exact predictions can be made in any particular case when a law is applied. The laws of psychology are statistically evolved, that is, they will predict what will happen to *most* people under the same conditions. Unfortunately, the Christian can never tell whether his contact falls in that general category. However, this is not too serious a disadvantage since most of our dealings *are* with average people.

But this proviso does mean that psychology should not be applied mechanically to evangelism. People are not machines to be operated at the whim of those who want to play God. They are persons made in God's image whose personalities must be respected.

This great truth establishes an ethics for evangelism. No tricks of psychology or of showmanship, good or bad, should be used to force a person to make a decision which is not the result of his free, unpressured will. It is no use arguing that dubious methods are all right because the purpose is his eternal salvation. The end does not justify the means. Not even God violates the human will.

The use of fringe areas of psychology to bypass the will are particularly obnoxious. Not only are such devices as hypnosis, hysteria, personality assault, and emotional shock insults to the person; they are useless. Conversion involves the conscious and deliberate surrender of the whole of the life in a manner designed to be permanent. Tricks can never accomplish that.

Since psychology is the study of behavior, the psychology of evangelism is the study of the behavior of the Christian and his contact when the former is seeking to bring about the latter's favorable response to the claims of Christ. It involves what both say, do, feel, react, and think. It also includes the changes which result in each, externally and internally, as the result of the confrontation.

In view of this explanation, there can be no question as to whether psychology is to be used in evangelism. It is merely a question of good psychology versus bad psychology. Wherever there is behavior, there is psychology. Without the aid of scientific psychology, this is liable to be inefficient, wasteful, and even harmful.

The science of psychology, with all its faults, inexactness, and immaturity due to the fact that man does not yet fully understand it, is one of God's good gifts. In the world of commerce its insights are continually enriching mankind. Jesus says we are to be as wise as the men of the world and make friends of the "mammon of unrighteousness" (Lk 16:9). If we are going to make a successful impact upon our world, we must do just that.

2
PSYCHOLOGY AND EVANGELISM

DUE TO THE VAST difference of opinion in defining evangelism, it is advisable to explain this book's viewpoint. The best description of evangelism is in the Great Commission. In Matthew 28:19-20, Jesus gave His charge under these headings: (1) teach all nations, (2) baptize them, (3) teach them to do all that He commanded.

Mark's gospel makes it clear that teaching all nations is not the same as teaching them to do all that Christ commanded. That first charge is the proclamation of the good news (Mk 16:15), the "kerygma" which Paul explains is the announcement of the death, burial, and resurrection of Christ (1 Co 15:3-4). But this was never preached as a mere matter of academic interest. Clearly, the hearer was being challenged by it to believe and commit his life to Christ in faith.

Since this response would soon evaporate unless it was conserved, public confession of it and identification with the Christian fellowship were necessary. These were accomplished through baptism.

Finally, since committal to Christ involves committal to His way of living, the convert must be taught this way. But, like the preaching, this teaching is not academic. It presupposes a continual positive response so that the life is rebuilt on that foundation. "Therefore whosoever heareth these sayings of mine, and doeth them, I will liken him unto a wise man, which built his house upon a rock" (Mt 7:24).

Thus, evangelism is intended to be much more than persuading people to make decisions, and it covers much more than conversion. Jesus has in mind total change in being, a complete reorientation, a permanent "set" of the personality to His philosophy of living.

Nothing superficial or mechanical is involved. The idea that man can make a deal with God in which God provides a ticket to heaven if man believes certain things and carries out certain acts, is quite foreign to the New Testament. Citizenship in the kingdom of heaven is not like citizenship through naturalization on earth. Here, if you fulfill the requirements, a court will declare you a citizen, and then you can continue living the same as before. With God, the price is your self. The terms are absolute, unconditional surrender. You yield yourself to live His way or He cannot receive you. No wonder becoming a Christian has never been popular.

However, the New Testament is also emphatic that this revolution in living does not result from mere self-effort. The response is human, as are the cooperation and self-giving, but the motivation and power are divine. In John 3, Jesus speaks of the Christian life as a kind of spiritual pregnancy wherein the Holy Spirit impregnates the human personality. The revolution is from within: the permeation of the human by the Divine, gradually molding it to the divine pattern. The Christian is not only a changed being but a new being.

If the work of evangelism is this far-reaching and revolutionary, the psychology involved obviously must be more than the door-to-door-salesman type where one is persuaded on the spur of the moment to buy a vacuum cleaner that he doesn't want. The furthest depths of the personality have to be reached so that the whole being is permanently affected. The theory of the unconscious may be the most useful in this respect. Although the psychoanalytic approach is now somewhat passé, and indeed always did have its faults, in this respect it is distinctly helpful.

Psychology and Evangelism

The basic presupposition of this theory is that we are creatures of our pasts. Jung even went so far as to suggest that even our racial past had a hand in determining our personalities before we were born. The events of life from birth onward are never really forgotten. They just go beyond our powers of immediate memory recall. They are all stored in the mind and this is known as the "unconscious."

These stored-up memories are by no means passive and dead. They remain alive with the emotions that originally activated them: fears, wishes, joys, anxieties, hungers, drives. Many of these emotions are very primitive and are, therefore, unacceptable to our adult, cultural, or religious standards and are unconsciously repressed. As pressure grows, outlet is found in the fantasies of dreams and daydreams, but most of all in the general direction which is given to living. We are not usually aware of this pressure, but it does generally provide the "set" for what we become.

Actually, this is not as deterministic as it sounds, although many psychoanalysts have made it appear so. There is always the human will which, within limits, has the power of self-determination regardless of the pressure of our past. Plato illustrated this distinction by comparing the psychological nature to a team of spirited horses, with the direction in which the horses were going being determined by the man with the reins: the human will.

Although the human will has this sovereign power, it get really tough when the "set" of the personality is in another direction. Some of us less-experienced horsemen have witnessed this when we have tried to direct a horse in one direction when he wanted to go in another, particularly when he wanted to go home!

Evangelism seeks to bring about a complete reorientation of the life. To be successful, therefore, it has to reach more than the will. It has to conquer the unconscious. This is quite a task and gets harder as a person gets older.

From the beginning of life the personality is egocentric. All the great physical and psychological drives are directed toward the pleasures and fulfillment of self. At first this self-centeredness is naked and unashamed, but after a while, parents and teachers try to civilize it a little. They really only succeed in driving it underground. The upshot of all this is that the natural unconscious is quite alien to God and His demands for self-giving. Perhaps this is the psychological counterpart of what the theologian calls "original sin."

During childhood it is relatively easy to change the orientation of the self; but unfortunately, it is just as easy for it to change back. Hence, the instability of youth. With increasing age the "set" of the personality becomes more pronounced, making change more difficult, but also making relapse more difficult too.

This is like inertia in physics. If you make a door out of three-ply lumber, you can move it with your finger; but if you make a massive door for a bank vault, it may require a motor to budge it. The very accumulation of experience in life increases the psychological inertia.

To make a decision for Christ isn't too hard. A person can can be made to see that this is in the best interest of the self, and the will may OK it. But unless some work has already been done on the unconscious, the whole "set" of the personality will be pulling in the opposite direction, creating an almost insufferable burden. This is why so many converts give up.

When I became a Christian at thirteen, I found Christianity the most unnatural thing in the world. It demanded that I do things that I didn't want to do, and it challenged me to action which I disliked. With the passage of the years that has altered. For all this time the influences on my unconscious have been predominantly Christian, giving a "set" to my personality in the way I want to go. As a result, to live as a Christian is far more "natural" now.

At first it might seem that living as a Christian would mean repression of the self, thereby building up an underground resistance movement in the unconscious against the Christian way. This sometimes does happen, especially under legalistic definitions of our faith, but it need not. In my case, I have been subjected to very little repression. I have sublimated and redirected my basic psychological needs so that they have found much greater fulfillment in Christ than they ever would in naked, direct self-seeking.

There is more to this. God's impregnation of the human spirit at conversion means that His gradual saturation of the personality becomes possible. It is by no means automatic. We have to consciously and continually give ourselves to Him in order for this permeation to occur. To the extent that this happens, the unconscious becomes reeducated and reoriented toward God by the power of His life within.

For the conversion experience to be meaningful and permanent, apparently it is necessary for the personality to be set toward God and the new way of living at the time of conversion. But since this is the point of entry of God into the life and the beginning of His permeation, such an orientation seems impossible at first.

Actually, a lot of spade work has gone on before this, or conversion would hardly have been possible anyway. What has been happening has been the long process which William James calls "subconscious incubation." As a result of the Holy Spirit's action on the life, the unconscious has been continually bombarded by spiritual impulses, especially if the person has been within hearing of the radioactive Word of God. His response may have been negative and his attitude indifferent, but his unconscious has not remained unmoved. An example of this is evident in the apostle Paul. Christ told him it was hard for him to kick against the goads. Even this fanatical, murderous, close-minded man had been nearer to Christ than he realized.

Apparently what happens is that the buildup of these positive elements in the inner personality continues until the weight counterbalances the negative egocentric impulses; then there is a switch of orientation, sometimes sudden and violent, but always enough to back up the decision of the will. If this process of incubation has not matured sufficiently, the decision of the will is likely to be premature and ineffective.

This does not mean that these impulses toward God-orientation have to be religious. In many cases they are not. The Christian ethic has so permeated our society that even nonchristian people exercise many of the Christian virtues toward one another.

The very needs of suffering people presuppose the value of human self-giving. All this tends to counterbalance the self-centered set of the personality. This is why a man with a negligible religious background may experience a conversion with complete personal change. His spiritual rebirth gives meaning and purpose to that which he recognizes as having been building up within him all the time.

Thus the study of the unconscious puts evangelism in its true perspective as a long process that affects man's deepest being. Unless adequate work has already been done on the unconscious, any hit-or-miss, one-shot attempts to bring about a decision will be meaningless. If, however, the preparation has been adequate, a single challenge may very well be all that is required to trigger off the spiritual revolution. But even then it must not be left there. The new personality orientation must be reinforced and made permanent by subsequent buildup of spiritual factors. Then the whole man will belong to God, and his evangelization will be complete.

3

THE INDIVIDUAL BEYOND HIS OWN SKIN

THUS FAR we have considered the individual in terms of what he is inside himself. Initially it may appear that this is all there is to a man: that his skin is the boundary of his being. But this is far from the truth. His personality reaches out to the environment in which he lives and, most particularly, to the persons who inhabit that environment.

This interaction with others is by no means accidental, in the sense that it occurs just because they happen to be there. The existence of others is necessary to his being. The very fact of his physical existence depends upon others. He comes into the world at the initiative of others and in the early years of childhood his life is completely dependent on others. That dependence lessens but never ceases throughout life.

The psychological tie with our fellow human beings is just as critical. We need people for love, companionship, mental stimulus, personality outreach, personal fulfillment. When we fail to find a satisfying life with others we wither and die, and life becomes impossible.

Any evangelism, therefore, that treats man as a detached individual and does not consider him in relationship to others will be geared to a completely false situation. It will find it hard to reach him in the first place and, even if it does, will not be able to lay claim to his total life, such as conversion demands.

Actually, the situation is even more complicated than that of a man interacting with other men in an individual-to-individual relationship. Man exists in social units such as family, marriage, societies, community, nation. He reacts differently to people within the units to which he belongs than he does to those outside these units, and he causes these units to interact with one another in ways which may vitally affect his own life.

Apparently the most basic unit of society is the family. It is the social cocoon in which the child is born and brought up and from which he emerges to get married and establish a family of his own. The family is an ideal setup in which a person can find the fulfillment of his most immediate and pressing physical, psychological, mental, and spiritual needs. A child deprived of a family is in deep personal peril. He feels lost and unable to adjust to others who do not have this misfortune. We realize this danger so urgently that we place him as quickly as possible in a foster home or an orphanage designed to be a substitute family.

In the Old Testament the cohesion between a person and his family was so close that he nearly ceased to have any rights as a person apart from his family. If a member of his family, particularly his father, committed a sin, the family as a whole was considered guilty; and, in capital cases, the whole family could be executed. The individual did not make his own decisions. The family made them for him. He was completely expendable in the interests of the family. When the time came for him to emerge to a family of his own, the choice of his mate was made for him. It is no wonder that the Old Testament has little to say about individual salvation. In this kind of context, individual existence has little meaning.

By New Testament times, some of this cohesion was broken down. Individual responsibility before the law and before God was fully recognized. A person was no longer completely expendable in the interests of his family. He had a greater loyalty to God. But the family unit was still strong, and there is strong evidence that evangelization was that of families rather than merely of individuals.

Usually it started with individuals, generally the head of the house. But when he believed, he brought his family into the church as well. We fondly hope that he persuaded each one individually to accept Christ too, but in those autocratic days they may not have had much say in it. This, of course, included the slaves which were in his household.

It is noticeable that when the Philippian jailor was baptized it was quickly added "and all his," that is, his family (Ac 16:33). This was done "straightway." No time was given to the individual members to think it over. His decision was good for the family and that was that.

There seems to be little doubt that the earliest churches were simply Christian families, "the church which is in thy house." This did not merely mean that the church used a house as its meeting place, but that the household was the church: parents, children, relatives, and slaves—although other individuals sometimes joined them. The idea of churches as corporations of individuals, or of families meeting in a building dedicated to the purpose, was a much later development.

Actually, the family always has been considered a unit within the church fellowship, even by those of us who do not baptize infants. In some churches we "dedicate" them, by which we signify—whether intentionally or not—that they are at least associated in some form with the church. Even where this is not done, the practical effects are the same. The child goes to Sunday school, worship services, and youth groups, and is deeply involved in the life of the church. Becoming a "member" adds little to this except that perhaps then he can vote and may become an "officer." From the strictly psychological or sociological point of view, if he is in a Christian family he is generally in the church life because of his family.

The breaking down of the cohesion within the family has greatly accelerated in our time. But it is interesting to note that where this disintegration is new, as in Japan, it is being accompanied by a marked rise in juvenile deliquency. Apparently our young people are hitting back at a society which has robbed them of the personal security that could be found only in the traditional family unit.

On the other hand, most young people welcome the new individual freedom. But whether it is good or bad, the family is now a *loosely* knit association of individuals.

This social development has enormously increased the difficulty of the task of evangelism. All we had to do once was to win the heads of the families, and the rest were shepherded almost automatically. Let us not assume that this follow-the-leader method was superficial either. Of course it could be, but more often than not, the other members of the family accepted the father's initiative and made significant personal committal to Christ. (The myth that family conversions were unreal is as untrue as the myth that "arranged" marriages were unhappy and loveless.)

Of course, for the children in the tight family unit, their personal acceptance of the Christian faith depended on their increasing maturity. But since they were under the control of the family until they emerged for marriage, they remained under the chuch's influence during those critical early teens. Since this is the age when most converisons occur, the probability that they would experience conversion was very great. That is, the family unit within the church was a great help toward continuing evangelization.

With the present weakening of family ties, the young person asserts his individualism in his early teens and uses his independence to disassociate with the church. He therefore misses the influence of the gospel at the very time when it is most likely to win him. More often than not he is permanently lost to the Christian faith.

There is not much that we can do about this social change; it is certainly here to stay. But we must recognize that evangelism now has to resort to the far more laborious process of winning individuals, one at a time.

But I do not think that we must assume that the possibility of family evangelism has gone. The family must always be the social unit which is vital to human security and happiness. What has happened is that the members emerge now at an earlier age rather than at the time of marriage, as previously. But up until the early teens, although the cohesion is weaker, it is still a psychological necessity. We should, therefore, direct our energies toward bringing the family into the orbit of the church's life, when the conversion of the mother or father occurs.

At this point we can get into trouble if we do not distinguish between the "church life" in the sociological sense and the "church" in the theological meaning. Theologically the church is the body of all those who have consciously committed themselves to Christ and received the indwelling of His Spirit. But the church life is a social *mixture*. It not only contains the spiritually reborn, but children and even more-or-less interested adults who are being nurtured toward this point of decision. The more a family is involved in this church life, the greater will be the chance of conversion of the people in it and the more likely the decisions will be conserved.

All this adds up to the fact that the person to be won for Christ is an individual-in-a-group or an individual-needing-a-group. Therefore his evangelization can only be meaningful in that setting.

This psychological fact confronts the pastor with two basic relative responsibilities: (1) he must do what he can to promote family cohesion; (2) he must make the church either a substitute family or a kind of second family.

By strengthening family ties in the families where the parents are Christians, he will be greatly increasing the pull toward Christ on the part of the children. The bond with the parents will tend to draw them into the same spiritual orbit as the parents. This is of necessity a long-range job and therefore should be a carefully planned element in the pastor's preaching, counseling, and administrative program.

Family cohesion depends on two factors, one negative and one positive. The ties loosen if there is lack of rapport in the home, bickering, misunderstanding, and selfishness. They tighten if there is love, concern for each other, and a sense of divine mission.

Success here depends partly on teaching. People must be made to know that disharmony among the members of the family is sinful, and that this must always be a primary area of Christian conquest.

Christianity, as a way of living, must start in the home. Each member should be powerfully aware that his faith demands the laying down of his own rights in the interest and the welfare of the others. Sermons and Sunday school lessons should be directed toward developing this kind of conscience.

Pastoral visitation will tend to drive this home, for it will give the pastor an opportunity to get to know the specific problems which he can then seek to solve by counseling. It cannot be done by the pulpit alone.

Program-planning should highlight the importance of the family by the setting up of functions especially for the family, such as church family dinners, family camps, and cottage meetings.

The question of family devotions should be handled with great care. If the children feel that this is being imposed on them, or if they find it burdensome, it will have a negative impact. This can be avoided by having the children take part themselves and by keeping the exercises short.

However, the needed factor for a Christian home is not so much religious as spiritual, not so much Christian services as

Christian service. The home can never be truly Christian unless it is a living example of Christ's philosophy of living.

The second responsibility of making the *church* a family means developing the New Testament ideal. This is important for the members of a closely knit human family, but it is absolutely vital for those in disintegrating families or those who have no families at all. People must be made to feel that they belong to the church and are not merely attached to it.

Unless the church is quite small, an intermediate step is needed to bridge the gap between the individual in his family and the individuals within the church. Otherwise the church is too big to be *emotionally* comprehended, and that is what counts. This intermediate step is the integration into smaller groups such as classes, youth fellowships, women's guilds, and men's societies. Experience shows that it is not enough just to make these available and to invite people to join them. The pastor must make sure that his contacts are carefully shepherded toward the group until the group's social adhesive takes over.

But a church or group is still not a family. In fact, it can degenerate into competitive cliques. These groups must be so integrated into the total life of the church that they see their existence only in terms of the church's welfare.

What has been said above about the importance of the family situation as a factor in evangelism applies most particularly to the husband-wife relationship. The Bible is very realistic about the fact that a married person is more than an individual and it refers to the married couple as being "one flesh." Although it is true that each partner must make his or her own decision to commit the life to Christ, such a decision cannot fail radically to affect the other person.

Paul felt so deeply about this that, in spite of his views on the sanctity of marriage, he said that a non-Christian partner had the right to depart if the spouse had become a Christian (1 Co 7:15). The incompatibility can be that serious.

The reason is that both marriage and religion reach very deeply into the life. Unless the married partners are also one at the spiritual level, there can be no real unity at all. The married person, if the marriage means anything, is no longer a separate individual.

The winning of one married partner without the other is therefore distinctly divisive. Since a person's own soul must come first, such a division may be necessary but should be avoided if at all possible. Couples should be encouraged to make their decisions together.

In seeking to win a married man or a woman, the pastor must resist the temptation to treat the contact as an individual, any more than he would treat a Siamese twin on his own. The married person is "one flesh" with someone else. He is part of a sociological and spiritual unity. This makes the job of evangelism much more complex, but it is the only realistic position to take. Of course, each partner must necessarily make a personal decision, good only for himself, but this should come about by winning the *total marriage* for Christ.

If the marriage itself is sick, this becomes the focal point of approach for the pastor. The partners must be made to see clearly what Christian marriage involves in this particular case, and how their own personal regeneration is related to it. Their surrender to Christ will then largely comprise their obedience to what Christ wants them to do to remake the marriage. There will be other factors too, not related to the marriage, but the marriage problem will give focus and sustenance to the decision to be made.

Where one partner is already a Christian, the pastor needs a two-pronged approach. The Christian must be made to see that his task goes far beyond that of talking his partner into becoming a Christian. The biblical requirement is to *be* a witness, rather than just to witness. The Christian must be a living example of the faith he is trying to promote.

When this is actually happening, the non-Christian partner

The Individual Beyond His Own Skin

can then be encouraged to become part of this Christian-marriage-in-embryo. The commitment to Christ will, as described above, be defined in terms of that relationship.

The Christian ideal of marriage, which is so crucial to winning married couples, is shown most clearly by actual example, most obviously by couples already in the church. The pastor, therefore, will do well to bring the couple he is trying to win into close contact with Christian couples.

Some churches have made quite a specialty of married-couple evangelism. They have a society for the purpose which generally runs a Bible class and social events. Member couples contact other couples and first bring them into the orbit of the church through the social activities. Once they get the feeling that they belong, the other step to discipleship is not too difficult.

But what of the unmarried person who is not part of a family or social group? Can he be treated as an individual? No. He is a person under tension, and he will remain that way unless he finds a satisfying family-type relationship. That may be difficult if his isolation is due to personality oddities, as it often is. If this is the case, the first step in winning him may well be counseling, helping him to adjust and win for himself meaningful relationships with others.

If the trouble is circumstances, for example, bereavement, the loving care and encouragement of the pastor will be especially needed. This is an excellent opportunity for the church members to close ranks around the sufferer, so that he may sense once again, even though in a much smaller way, the security of being part of the group. Once that has been achieved, the path to winning him is much easier.

The whole church should be alerted to these group needs, in the New Testament phrase, "given to hospitality." It costs something to invite strangers into our homes, but evangelism always has been costly.

But apart from a person's family relationships, he cannot be a Christian just in himself. His spiritual life presupposes an association with other Christians. The convert needs the Christian family. In this respect the interdenominational evangelistic crusade often fails because it wins a man as an individual without regard to a wider relationship. Instead of being born again in a church, he must go and find one. This has all the defects of an orphan in a foster home.

Most evangelists are now seriously facing this problem. Shepherding and follow-through are generally considered as an integral part of the evangelistic process. This is vitally necessary. According to some figures I have seen (whose validity I have no way of testing) the expected loss of converts from mass meetings is 97 percent. In view of the psychological facts discussed in this chapter, I would not be surprised.

All this outlines the need for the church to be a cohesive, loving fellowship. Perhaps this is why the New Testament appeals so urgently for unity and has such a horror of divisiveness. It is tragic to see fellowship spoiled by well-meaning people nit-picking on points of doctrine or procedure. "Straining at a gnat and swallowing a camel," is what Jesus called it.

The pastor who can succeed in developing this love and unity within the church will, psychologically and spiritually, be creating a favorable climate for evangelism.

The best kind of evangelism is the "spontaneous combustion" variety where the atmosphere is so God-filled that people *volunteer* to become Christians. This will occur when the deepest group needs of people are being met. Edwin Orr has stated that almost every revival (outpouring of the Holy Spirit in conversions) has been characterized by Christians getting right with God and therefore with the brethren.

4

THE BASIC DRIVE

IN OUR PSYCHOLOGICAL DESCRIPTION of the person so far we have discovered that he is a complex product of his past experiences interacting with his environment, especially with other people. It must now be added that this behavior is not aimless or merely subject to the surrounding influences. He is not like an unmanned boat at the mercy of the vagaries of wind and wave. He is like a ship with powerful engines set on a definite course independent of the elements.

This does not mean that he knows where he is going as far as life is concerned. He seldom does. To use the same analogy, he is not like a ship heading toward a definite port. He is more like a ship hunting for whales. He may not know *where* they are but he does know *what* he is looking for.

Of course man has a large number of instinctual drives, some physical; some psychological, such as hunger, thirst, sex, sleep, self-protection, self-assertion; some social; love, and many others. Each of these is seeking gratification, but not in isolation, unless the need becomes extreme. Generally there is an overriding framework which determines how the need is satisfied. The individual instinct is subordinated to the drive of the personality as a whole.

There was a time when psychology considered a person's motivation as being the sum total of a number of instincts, but it has long since been conclusively proved that this is not so. A man is not the sum of anything. He isn't a collection. He is a person and acts as a whole. His total being is in action, and his motivation in living must be understood accordingly.

This is sometimes known as the gestalt principle. The clearest illustration of this is in medicine. The modern physician does not merely treat symptoms; he treats the body as a whole. The symptoms indicate to him that there is something wrong with the *organism*. In many cases of illness, the doctor never knows what is wrong. He sees the evidences of some infection and knows that the organism has been invaded. When antibiotics stem this invasion, the symptoms disappear. But just imagine what would happen if a doctor merely put ointment on the sores when the patient had smallpox!

Applied to psychology, the gestalt principle means that we cannot understand a person by looking at his individual instincts. Neither can we cure his unhappinesses by mollifying his separate grievances. These are often just symptoms that show the personality itself is in trouble. Put that right and the symptoms may disappear. Yet, if we treat the symptoms alone, we may succeed in removing them, only to find that others take their place, because they are the personality's way of drawing attention to the fact that something is *basically* wrong.

For the purposes of this book it will be best to consider this basic inner drive as a craving for ego fulfillment. But "ego" must be taken more widely than its meaning in words like "egotistical," which have an unpleasant connotation. The ego is the "I," the person himself who is striving for self-realization in ways that may be good or bad.

The individual instincts such as those mentioned above are merely channels which the personality uses to gain fulfillment. The clearest example of this is sex. Beyond the physical sensation of pleasure is the ego satisfaction of power over another person or the thrill of the achievement of being able to win the partner's love.

Thus, any attempt to cure sexual problems by paying attention to sexual considerations only, would be doomed to failure. We would need to find out why the *personality* was causing the problem.

The presence of this personality drive means that from earliest childhood the person finds himself with abilities and powers which refuse to lie dormant and demand expression, regardless of the obstacles involved. In view of what already has been said about a man's not being an individual in himself but an individual-in-relation-to others, fulfillment can never be satisfied in isolation. It has to be recognized by other people.

As with all instincts, to ego fulfillment there is an accompanying emotion, or actually, a polarity of emotions: happiness-frustration. When we are finding adequate fulfillment and recognition we experience an emotional glow that we call happiness. But when this satisfaction does not occur, we are filled with frustration which can vary from a vague feeling of mental malaise to an agony of misery.

So close is the correlation between fulfillment and happiness that the principle becomes invaluable in counseling. Wherever we find human unhappiness or maladjustment we will also find that somewhere there is a blockage to personality fulfillment. Remove it and the glow of living will return. The result has been a swing from analysis to synthesis.

In analysis we dig into a person's past in the Freudian manner to find shocks that may have triggered off the problem. In synthesis, we seek to help the person to find a more adequate fulfillment and recognition. If this is achieved, the unhappiness and disturbance generally evaporate. Some of us have a sneaking suspicion that the chief value of psychoanalysis was in the interest shown in the patient, making him feel fulfilled and recognized. Be that as it may, the synthetic approach is much more direct and practical.

This drive for fulfillment is lifelong. It starts with the

infant long before he develops self-consciousness. The only expression he is capable of at that stage is physical, and apparently his personality finds its necessary satisfaction in that alone. Thus, suppression of this expression brings sharp emotional response. If someone holds his arms and legs so that he cannot move he will quickly show his frustration by rage.

When self-consciousness develops, the child has the difficult experience of attempting to satisfy his inner drive to achieve when he has no knowledge of the results that might follow his adventures. He is forced to act completely in the dark. If he is lucky enough to undertake something that his parents approve of he finds both fulfillment and recognition, and immediately his pleasure is evident. Often he has to be stopped for his own good when he is not so lucky. His frustration and distress are then pitiable to see.

When he goes to school, the odds against fulfillment are raised, for now he has to contend with many other persons who are themselves seeking to contend with many other persons who are themselves seeking their own satisfaction, often in open conflict with his own. If he has courage and initiative, he will still find his place in the sun. If he doesn't or if he is stopped by forces not under his control, there is the beginning of a maladjusted personality.

The teenager adds still another factor: a degree of independence. This increases the opportunities for fulfillment but also raises the risks. The obstacles are now formidable: physical, economic, personality; and the circumstances are more competitive than ever. If the young person surmounts them and achieves a satisfying life, he is happy and mature. If he fails, the frustration may impel him into pseudo-fulfillment such as delinquency. The fact that suicide is a major cause of death among teenagers is tragic witness to the extent of the misery that can result from this failure.

The happiness of adult life is largely determined by the same principle. A person will be happy and contented to the extent in which he is achieving satisfactorily the best he is capable of and when this is being recognized by those around him.

It was once assumed in industrial psychology that people just wanted more money and better working conditions. These are important, of course, but it has been shown time and time again that individuals will sacrifice these things for jobs where they can find more adequate self-expression or fulfillment.

Adjustment in marriage depends on the same rule. For happiness, each partner has to find his or her satisfying fulfillment within the limitations of marriage. Too much unity at the expense of personal fulfillment can be disastrous because it bottles up this inner drive. Sooner or later an explosion is inevitable.

Retirement is an especially dangerous period because it can leave a person with no adequate channels for self-expression. An active, physically well man may wither and die a few years after retirement if he does not have sufficient work to capture his imagination and to challenge his abilities.

There is no time throughout life when this drive is not operative. Fulfillment is always progressive. What satisfies me now will prove inadequate tomorrow. The very use of my inner powers causes them to grow and therefore demand even greater expression.

One of the sad things about life is that people drift out of fulfillment. They reach a point of self-expression which is adequate and then imagine they have it made. But soon the sense of challenge recedes and frustration begins to build up. Thus, apparently successful people fall victims to alcoholism and similar pseudo-satisfactions.

A good illustration of the truth explained in this chapter is in the parable of the talents. At first glance, the man who had one talent and buried it in the ground does not appear to be particularly sinful but just overcautious. Jesus' harsh words are therefore hard to understand until we realize just what the sin was. In failing to use his talent, the man robbed himself of an opportunity for self-fulfillment and, in so doing, robbed his master and his community as well. To Christ that was a terrible sin because it was an offense against the dignity of man made in the image of God.

The term "talent" now has come to mean a specific aptitude, such as being able to play a musical instrument. But the application is much wider. The talent is *all* the ability we have for self-expression. Not only our psychic well-being but our faithfulness to Christian commitment depends on it. In God's eyes, failure here is more than folly; it is sin.

This is where the "joy of the Lord" becomes possible. It is certainly not an automatic product of conversion, dropping like manna from heaven. It is a by-product of living out the implications of conversion. Commitment to Christ necessitates the using of all we have to the utmost in His service. When this happens, the glow of happiness is inevitable. Without this commitment the Christian, no matter how religious, may be more miserable than the non-Christian.

One of the great contributions of the Christian faith is that it helps us to conquer the greatest enemy to fulfillment, and that is inertia. We may know perfectly well that satisfying living comes from having all our potential under extension and yet we may take no step toward this. We may be just plain lazy or lacking in courage or initiative. Many people are quite unhappy this way; nevertheless, they prefer to stay in a rut rather than attempt the great adventure.

But when a person becomes a Christian—if he is really sincere about it—he renounces this inertia and determines to extend himself to the fullest for God. Indeed, the Spirit of God will give him no peace until he achieves this. He is constantly nudging us into the path of joy in spite of ourselves. This means that it is impossible for us to be committed Chris-

THE BASIC DRIVE

tians without being happy Christians. God has arranged things that way.

However, the life in Christ does much more for us than merely to provide the incentive to satisfied living. It assists in drawing out the potential from within. We are regenerated by the Holy Spirit, which means that we have an active principle within joined to our spirit which makes our capacity to achieve almost unlimited. United to God, we are right at the fountain of all creativity. The joy and satisfaction in living that can result are correspondingly almost infinite.

The relevance of evangelism to this basic drive is immediately apparent. If we can succeed in making a person aware that conversion promises a continuing satisfaction to this deepest need of his being, his inner pressure to become a Christian will be considerable.

Unfortunately most people haven't the faintest idea that the gospel promises this exciting possibility. Instead there are several popular misconceptions which blur the gospel appeal. It is often thought that the Christian faith is a deprivation of joy in living, or that it is a mere pattern of religious observances, or that it is a hair splitting system of beliefs. Christianity does involve some of these elements but they are only incidental. The modern evangelist has to sell the biblical point of view that the Christian faith is God's way to undreamed-of personal fulfillment. This will necessitate a shift to a more positive point of view in order to change this false but popular image of Christianity.

On the first problem most people still seem convinced that a religious faith is negative, a life of self-denial and deprivation. This is our heritage from previous Puritan and monastic eras which, in many ways, were a distortion of the Christian faith. Christ said that He came to bring life and that more abundantly (Jn 10:10), but often our message has been the very antithesis of this.

Of course, there is a negative side to Christianity, and there are prohibitions, self-denial, and some deprivation. But this is never arbitrary. It is always with a positive purpose in view: to protect people from unhappiness. The means may not be too pleasant at times, but the goal is always positive: the good life. This must be spelled out; where sin has to be denounced, it should be shown in its relation to what is to be gained.

Actually, it makes much better psychology not to denounce directly anyway. It is something like drumming into a child that he must not steal the candy. We can finish up by unintentionally talking him into it! This is called the law of reversed effort: the thing that you try too hard not to do, you end up doing.

The best approach is that illustrated in a common problem with children. If your child has a razor blade and you try to take it from him, he will resist and cut himself. But if you offer him candy, he will drop the blade to get it. Evangelistic preaching needs to focus on the candy!

A good case in point is the problem of premarital sex in young people. Blasting the practice will do no good. But we can reach them by showing that carelessness here robs marriage of its highest fulfillment later on.

But neither is there any attraction in a gospel which majors on religious observance. The religious ceremonies of any age are simply the social forms which express spiritual experience at that time. These quickly get out-of-date but tend to persevere nevertheless. This is the kind of thing which has bedeviled missionary work, whereby converts were forced to accept Western culture (and even Western dress) as a part of the Christian faith.

The form does not matter. The emphasis must be on the living experience of Christ whereby His Spirit enters the life and empowers for living.

Bare theological preaching is similarly unattractive. Many

proclamations of what is known as the "plan of salvation" suffer from this defect. People are given the impression that conversion consists of believing a certain explanation about the cross or accepting a set of beliefs. The trouble is that all this orthodoxy may be purely intellectual. Real faith is what we do with the whole life, not merely the mind. The Scriptures tell us to believe *in* Christ, not merely to believe Christ. That "believing in" calls for the committal of the whole life.

Christianity is a change of being, not just a change of mind. It is far more than a contract we make with God in exchange for which He gives us heaven when we die. It is the impregnation of our spirit by God so that He can give us power to overcome. That kind of preaching will always touch a responsive chord because it promises the fulfillment we crave for. The accent is on challenge—self-realization through a force greater than ourselves.

The Bible makes a tremendous appeal to the infinite possibilities of achievement when surrendered to God. Jesus Himself said: "Greater works than these shall he [the believer] do; because I go unto my Father" (Jn 14:12). Paul echoed this in his words: "I can do all things through Christ which strengtheneth me" (Phil 4:13). "Now unto Him that is able to do exceeding abundantly above all that we ask or think, according to the power that worketh in us" (Eph 3:20).

But even more encouraging than the statements of Scripture are the biblical stories. The Bible is full of accounts of people who faced impossible tasks and yet were empowered by God to carry them out successfully. For instance, Moses, at eighty years of age was called to deliver a nation of slaves from the mightiest military power on earth, and take them across a near-impassable wilderness to their promised land. His feeling of utter incapacity was evident at his call at the burning bush. But he succeeded anyway. Incredible successes like this are winsomely attractive to people struggling against heartbreaking odds to fulfill their dreams.

But since these events happened such a long time ago, there is a danger that people may think that they are no longer relevant, that such miracles could happen long ago but not now. It therefore pays to back up the biblical example by modern examples of similar achievements. When I was a boy, blocked by all kinds of obstacles and bedeviled by feelings of inferiority, I was fired by the accounts of great men like David Livingstone, Hudson Taylor, George Müller, and a host of others who achieved the impossible. Such stories made me want to be a Christian so that I could do the same.

Personally, I think that the teen years are the most painful years in a person's life. They are also the most exciting, too, of course. But the emergence into independent successful adult living can be terribly discouraging. The opportunity for evangelism in this particular respect is therefore particularly great.

But even in adulthood, this angle never loses its appeal. Witness to this are the successes of Norman Vincent Peale, Dale Carnegie, and the like, where the following has gone into many millions. The Christian gospel, wisely directed toward this need, can reap an unbelievable harvest.

So far I have limited this discussion on the relevance of this basic drive to the presentation of the gospel in order to gain the initial decision. But there is also an important application to conservation too.

Regardless of denominational differences in church government, most churches now encourage member participation in planning and executing the church's program. The result is not always efficiency in getting the job done, but it pays great dividends in the sense of fulfillment in the hearts of the members. To be relevant, a man's church is not only a place where he is taught how to find fulfillment in everyday life; it must also be its own satisfaction. If he is finding this in his church, it will mean that his vital psychological drive will have a stake in his continuing rather than drifting off.

The Basic Drive

This is especially important with young people. Programs made by others and handed to them on a platter will not hold them. They need to be encouraged to use their own initiative, to create the situations which they will find challenging and satisfying. Even in the teaching process, the more the truths are drawn out from youth themselves, the more acceptable they will be. I'm all for younger deacons and officers whereby young people can take an active part in determining their own religious environment. In all areas the church must cease to be something to be endured and become a vital adventure in self-realization.

Actually, fulfillment through participation does have a relevance to winning people in the first place as well as conserving them after they have been converted. This participation may be outside of the church as well as in its internal program.

I well remember a retired man who had made the mistake of retiring from a satisfying job without taking up something fulfilling to capture his imagination. His frustration was painful to both him and to his family. I was able to get him interested in a community service project in which he did an excellent job. In this fulfillment his frustration evaporated. He started coming to church and soon made his decision for Christ.

This kind of thing has happened many times. The implication is that if the pastor can lead people into more satisfying lives this will predispose them toward Christ. But the fulfillment can well be in the church's program itself. If you want to get a man interested, give him something to do which he likes and which will be fulfilling to him. A carpenter might put in a door, a gardner might plant a bed of roses, a banker might devise a financial scheme. Actually it is best if the talent to be used is a hobby because the regular task may have become burdensome anyway. A bonus from this kind of special services is its recognition by the church people, for this is always most satisfying to the ego.

The upshot of anything like this is the emotional feeling of well-being that results. It creates an atmosphere in which a person is amenable to the gospel.

Possible applications for this ego drive are unlimited. Once the pastor is aware of just how powerful this is, he can use his ingenuity to devise a thousand ways in which he can harness it to win people for Christ.

5
CAUSE HUNGER

AN INTERESTING EXTENSION of the basic drive described in the last chapter is what has been called "cause hunger." It is the compulsion to find fulfillment in a cause so demanding that it captures our whole being and makes us willing to make even the most expensive sacrifices on its behalf. It becomes the channeling of the "drive to achieve" toward a clearly defined goal.

As human beings, we cannot be happy if we just live, even if we are affluent enough to buy all the creature comforts. We have to have something to live *for*. We are born crusaders.

This is becoming particularly evident in our time as increasing economic security is robbing us of the most fundamental crusade of all: the struggle to find the necessary subsistence for ourselves and our families. Until recently this has monopolized almost the whole attention of man. There has been no choice about this, and it usually has been far from pleasant and fraught with anxiety, but nevertheless, the achievement of this very elementary goal brought deep personal satisfaction.

Our happy release from this bondage has left us as people without a cause. We have developed an uneasy feeling of aimlessness, a sense of being unneeded. As a result we are sitting ducks for any harebrained scheme that comes along. As TIME magazine has put it, we have become a "cause hungry" society.

We have become so hungry for a crusade that it has became ludricrous. In recent years there have been crusades to put trousers on animals, to use four-letter words in public, to make pedestrians wear red lights on the seats at nighttime, to allow workers to do a certain amount of pilfering.

Then there are the big crusades aimed at changing the structure of society itself: civil rights, abolition of capital punishment, outlawing of war, democratization of universities, eliminaiton of certain diseases like polio.

In all of the serious crusades there is a hard core whose main interest is in the problem concerned, but generally there are many others who are not so much concerned with the ultimate goal as with the process of being involved in fighting for *something*. Often when their causes lose momentum, they will readily switch to something else. These are the "mercenaries" of the crusades; only, their pay is not money but the satisfaction of driving for a cause—any cause.

So widespread is this phenomenon of "cause hunger" that it is fast becoming a commercial product. Certain organizations can now be hired to organize a crusade, complete with demonstrations, publicity, and the other trappings which are fast developing a stereotyped form.

Not only is this cause-hunger effect becoming more and more widespread geographically and over every aspect of living, it is also increasing rather alarmingly in depth. The drive to realize a crusade's goal is becoming so powerful that violence is being resorted to. In many instances all sense of proportion has been lost. The very fabric of law and order, without which no society can continue to exist, is being sacrificed for the gaining of ends which can have no meaning without law and order.

The author is not so much concerned here with the beneficial and the detrimental aspects of the various crusades, but would only point out that, for good or ill, the crusading spirit is part of our world and, therefore, it can be used profitably in the process of evangelism. Actually, the more "cause hunger" is used up in this constructive way, the less it will find outlet in destructive channels.

Thus far in this study it has been obvious that Christianity has been tailor-made to fit the needs of man's psychological nature. Christian faith is incurably a crusading religion. Throughout the Bible there is a constant call, usually in the most urgent tones, to commit oneself, regardless of the sacrifice involved, to the divine task to which God Himself has set His face.

Actually this is the crux of the whole matter. God is revealed as the great crusader Himself. His crusade is that of redemption, or—to use a more meaningful term now—rescue. The picture is that of mankind struck down by the terrible epidemic of sin with all its disastrous results in human suffering, heartbreak, and misery. God, grieved beyond all comprehension by this stark tragedy, is desperately trying to rescue man by offering him the remedy and by alleviating the suffering involved.

In Old Testament times this rescue operation was expressed through the heartrendering endeavors of great men of God who became identified with the divine vision. The crusade reached its climax in the life and death of Jesus when God Himself entered this stricken world. It has continued ever since in the work of the Holy Spirit who seeks to apply the work of Christ as an antibiotic to human sin and to minister to the distresses of those who have been struck by the plague.

Faith in Christ means identification with God in this rescue. Mere participation is not enough. An involvement of the whole being is required to the extent that we feel the same heartache and terrible urgency that God feels. Only then can we have the necessary motivation to drive us to the self-giving and sacrifice that are inevitable in such a struggle.

In the early days of the church this picture was cruelly clear. Committal to Christ then involved the danger of fiendish torture, rotting imprisonment, the agonizing loneliness of exile, and death in excruciating horror. Yet, at that time, the appeal of Christianity was never more attractive. The convert classes were thronged with eager supplicants. Life and death took on a significance so crystal clear that even the most terrible sacrifices seemed trifling in comparison.

The really exciting times of Christian history have always been when Christian missions have taken on a specific new aspect. The Reformation was one of these times. Then the vision was of a church rescued from corruption and empty formalism to regain New Testament vitality. The modern missionary movement was another. The conscience of the Christian world was awakened to the unevangelized millions still wallowing in primeval savagery. The effect was electric. Young people by the thousand eagerly committed themselves to this thrilling cause, even though it meant the probability of premature death or disablement. The missionary meetings during the heyday of that era became the most fruitful venue for evangelism.

Unfortunately, we are not now living in one of these great new departures in the Christian mission. Instead, we have the steady job of implementing the Christian faith without the fireworks of a new rocket in the sky. The terrible need for human redemption is still there, but there is no specific crusade of such urgency that it stands out in the full glare of publicity and makes its own appeal automatically. To capture the imagination now, it has to be spelled out until those we seek to win become so personally moved that they are fired to do something about it. They will commit themselves to Christ if they feel He is offering them a crusade that will satisfy the craving to have something significant to strive for.

Recently in Honolulu I met with a number of students

who were really fired with the work of evangelism. I noticed that they were cleverly exploiting the cause-hunger unrest all around them. Their catchword was "Help us to change the world." They were enthusiastic about the New Testament idea of changing the world by changing people through the transforming power of the Spirit of Christ within the life.

They were smart enough to realize that an appeal to commitment to Christ on the grounds of personal salvation alone would not stir a ripple of interest. Yet, when personal salvation was shown to be a step in a cause greater than themselves, it had immediate appeal.

There was a time when the crusade spirit was directed toward saving souls in terms of the life to come. General William Booth of the Salvation Army won thousands of recruits, not on the basis of their own release from the danger of being lost souls, but on his stirring appeal to rescue other souls from hell. With changing times that slant is no longer effective. It is not that Christians have lost their faith in the hereafter. It is just that people now are moved by crusades that are directed to the here and now.

You challenge a person to become a Christian so that he can save souls from hell and he will remain unmoved, but appeal to him to commit himself to Christ to help Him in His rescue operation and he will listen. The switch from saving "souls" to saving "people" is mute but healthy witness to this change.

Whether a crusade has appeal seems to depend largely on three factors: the significance, the sense of urgency, and the specificness. Significance depends upon what the crusade can accomplish and especially on what will happen if the crusade does not succeed. Urgency is a time factor. It comes from the need to do something *now*. Specificness is determined by the extent in which the action and the goals of the crusade are clearly defined. For instance, a movement to "help the poor" has no cutting edge, but a drive to provide school lunches for underprivileged children is sharp and appealing.

Applying these principles to the Christian message, we can see it has built-in appeal. It is significant both for the individual and society. The Christian faith in the New Testament sense not only tells how life should be lived; it gives the power to do so. When a person is fully surrendered to Christ, the power within begins to drive out the undesirable things and replace them by the fruit of the Spirit. All around us there are beaten discouraged people who desperately need a gospel like this. Psychology, education, counseling: all these things can help them, but only Christ can save. Even to the best of men, life without Christ realizes only a mere fraction of its potential. The Christian evangelist is the carrier of *good news* indeed.

The Christian point of view has always been that a changed society is impossible without changed men. This means that no matter how desperately our social engineers seek to remake our world, they will find the task hopeless unless enough human hearts are changed. This applies to homes, marriages, towns, nations, and the whole world.

Failure to realize this has brought great discouragement to our age. This century started with high hopes that our great discoveries would solve our social problems. Instead, it has been a century of unprecedented bloodshed, increase of crime, and a snowballing of human problems. The reason is that only Christianity can get deep enough into the human heart to make the necessary basic changes. The social failure of the twentieth century has been the failure of evangelism. Instead of our faith being irrelevant to our age it is the most significant factor in mankind's survival.

On the second point of urgency, things could not be more critical. Every minister in any large city can testify to the desperate human misery which assaults him on every hand. The thing that breaks down the health of so many ministers is the weight of the responsibility that they often stand between life and death. If they fail, they know the result will be suicide, murder, broken homes, prison perhaps.

The trouble is that many of our own members, let alone those out in the world, do not know of this human tragedy. If the evangelist can succeed in showing Christianity in this light, there will be no question of the urgency of the Christian quest.

Actually, the scientific revolution has vastly increased this sense of urgency. In bygone days, human wickedness has wrought incredible suffering, but now that evil can be armed with atomic bombs the possibilities are too horrible to contemplate. Only the message of Christ stands between man and his ultimate destruction. Unless we evangelize the world, human sin will destroy it. The man who accepts Christ, by so doing, stands with others between mankind and its doom. It is just that urgent.

On the third point of specificity, the Word of God tracks human problems down to a person's own selfishness and sin. Anger is the root of murder, lust is the cause of sexual moral disease, selfishness destroys marriages, deceit ruins mutual trust, greed germinates poverty and war. It is not circumstances that ruin lives, not even sin in general, but *my* sin: my anger, my lust, my selfishness, my lies.

According to the Christian message, I am the traitor to God selling out to the devil. But all this can be remedied within my own spirit by the divine antibiotics of the indwelling Spirit who enters at conversion.

The non-Christian has to see himself in this framework. He is to be redeemed so that he may redeem, not merely by his words or actions, but by the impact of his life. He must see himself making beachheads on the entrenchments of evil in his own life, his home, his job, his community.

Unfortunately, the church does not always show this crusading spirit. It appears to the outsider as dull, moribund, petty, uninvolved. It is hard to convince him that its whole soul is caught up in the work of redemption when most of its money goes into bricks and mortar and overhead, when little of the time of its minister is spent on the Christian mission itself. Anything that can be done to bring the church back to the task which God has given it to do, will enormously boost the evangelistic appeal.

It must not be inferred from all this that Christian action is merely within the heart. This is where the root of the problem lies, but the Christian faith is not only an onslaught on the roots of sin, but also on its unhappy consequences. Jesus not only preached the need of the changed heart; He also went about doing good. Those who follow Him must be constantly making beachheads on human suffering wherever it is found.

The world can never be saved in general. The work can only be done by millions of Christians each trying to win individuals for Christ and by small groups of Christians in limited areas taking on small projects for the kingdom of God.

Redemption will have no practical meaning for the members of a church unless it is being exemplified in actual operations which they can see and in which they can participate. On the direct evangelistic side this will involve visitation, evangelism campaigns, or the promotion of special meetings. But indirectly it may call for such projects as planned hospital visitation, schemes to make life better for shut-ins and the aged infirm, lifeline services for those in emergencies, programs for youth and the like. Churches which are really concerned about human suffering will survey their neighborhood to make sure that no area of human need escapes their attention.

Christianity in action under the right leadership is always effective evangelistically. It appeals to the crusading spirit in people and draws them in. However, to win people for Christ, Christian action does not need to be confined to a spectator operation where outsiders see Christians at work. It is much more effective as an evangelistic pull if the non-Christian is involved himself. Once he participates with other Christians in a crusade like this, he will feel something of the heartthrob of redemption himself. In a sense, he will *feel* the message of Christ, not merely listen to it.

The crusade element is vitally important in the approach to young people, especially now. They will despise us if we insult their dignity by trying to bribe them by entertainment. On one occasion a clergyman approached one of the Beatles to get the group to sing at a church function. The Beatle refused, saying, "You don't need us. You need to improve your product!"

If this crusade spirit is to remain effective, it must be backed up by actual deeds. People must know of the action. They must be aware of the advances in missionary endeavor at home and abroad. They must witness the conquests for God in their own church area. They must be aware of the social action going on. They must be challenged by the promotion of a constant stream of responsible plans for outreach. Essentially the crusade spirit is an atmosphere, exciting yet demanding.

Although this chapter has dealt with the divine mission of the church, very little has been said about man's eternal destiny which traditionally has been the focal emphasis of the message. The reason for this neglect is that the doctrine of the hereafter no longer carries the evangelistic appeal that it used to. In this book we are concerned with that aspect only.

However, every pastor should keep in mind that this doctrine cannot simply be left out in today's preaching. The life-after-death element is absolutely essential if the life-now emphasis is to be made meaningful. Part of the significance of the gospel message is that we are *eternal* beings and are being prepared for an *eternal* destiny.

The reason why heaven-and-hell preaching fell into disrepute is because it was often out of all context with living now. But present-day relevance and future destiny are not mutually exclusive alternatives.

What we need are balance and a positive approach. If we followed the balance of the New Testament we would have no problem. Paul strongly emphasizes the importance of the hereafter, but it is usually only a by-product of his general message. He doesn't make the mistake of crying wolf *all* the time.

The positive approach is highly desirable. The negative appeal to fear as a motivation has lost any effectiveness that it ever had. The Bible gives us no details about the life to come, but it does give the impression that it is an experience of unparalleled opportunity with earthly limitations removed. That makes for an exciting frosting on the here-and-now cake.

6
THE DRIVE TO BELONG

MAN IS A SOCIAL BEING who cannot happily exist alone. Occasionally we hear of a hermit who spends his life in abstemious solitude, but we shudder at the thought. Obviously we are made by God to live out our lives with others.

The drive is only partly for companionship, although that is very evident too, especially when we haven't seen anyone for a while. It used to be very noticeable in pioneer settlements such as in the Australian Outback. In her classic book, *We of the Never Never,* Mrs. Aeneaus Gunn tells of the excitement about the monthly visits of the mail carrier, who was welcomed like a prince, not just because he brought news of the outside world, but because he was company.

The Rev. John Flynn, the famous Presbyterian minister who did so much for the Outback, made good use of this hunger for companionship. Making the rounds of the scattered, isolated sheep-and-cattle stations, where the only roads were dirt tracks, involved terrible hardships, but it was these very conditions which made him so valuable to those lonely people. His message was welcome because he was.

Radio, TV, the airplane and other products of modern technology have altered all that, not only in Australia but in most other lands as well. Now the drive just to have people around is no longer pressing. Indeed, we are often more anxious to get away from people. The day is long gone when an itinerant evangelist would have been welcome even if he had two heads.

But the social instinct is much deeper than the desire to be with people. Evidence of this is the loneliness that we may experience in a strange city. There may be millions of people around us yet we may feel terribly alone. This is because we do not *belong*.

This need to belong is far more powerful than the need merely to have people around. Apparently we are driven irresistibly to come into such close relationships with groups that we become important to them and they to us. Fortunately for the work of the gospel, this is a need which will remain quite independent of technological advance.

The drive to belong seems to be closely associated with the basic ego drive expounded in chapter 4. We have to feel important and needed, not only to people at large, but to a group or groups, even though the group may comprise only two people. This can never be superficial if we are going to be satisfied. We must feel that we are absolutely necessary to the welfare and happiness of others besides ourselves. We must be convinced that they care so much about us that they are as anxious about us as they are about themselves.

This amounts to a mutual-anxiety state but of the most pleasant kind. It involves an element of worry and the possibility of being hurt, but we feel it is certainly worth it. *Belongingness* is a state of emotional integration.

The characteristic emotion of belongingness is love. Love occurs in its most intense form in maternal love and sexual love, but these can be self-defeating unless they are backed up by that more general love that can be true of any other relationship as well. This general love is the *feeling* of belongingness, that spiritual integration with another person or other people that becomes so important that the self is committed to it regardless of the personal cost involved. This is one of the most essential needs of human beings. Christianity strongly emphasizes belongingness and therefore is ideally tailored to human need.

The Christian doctrine of God appeals powerfully to this need. This is seen most especially in the teachings of Jesus. God is the heavenly Father deeply interested in human need. We belong to Him because we are His children. He is so interested in us that even the very hairs on our heads are numbered. He suffers with us when we suffer.

Paul has a lot to say in the same strain about the indwelling Christ. At conversion the Holy Spirit enters the personality, and we become new creatures in union with God. This union persists even in and beyond death. We are so inseparably united to Him that we will always be where He is, whether in the fleshly body or outside it. Nothing can separate us from the love of Christ. We belong, eternally.

The theology of reconciliation in the New Testament presupposes this need to belong. Sin breaks the union with God and we cease to belong. From then on we are like homing pigeons seeking the home we have lost. Christ is the great Reconciler. He reconciles God to us and us to God so that once more we belong.

This is at the very heart of the gospel message, and the pastor will do well to major on it. Attractively presented, it will always bring a sympathetic response.

It is this drive to belong which makes marriage so important and generally so desirable. The cynic who views marriage as a license for sexual gratification is way off base, although that is obviously part of it. Indeed, those who are sexually promiscous often desire marriage the most. Neither is it the need for companionship. The bringing of unmarried young people into fellowship is a step in the right direction, but it is pathetically obvious that this is not what they really need.

Marriage is desired most because it promises the ultimate in belongingness. It brings us into a union with another person whose welfare will become so inextricably wound up with ours that our every hope and fear becomes of vital importance to her (or him). It is a secure nest where our emotional anxieties can rest and be at peace. In a happy and fulfilling marriage we really belong.

On the reverse side this is why a broken or out-of-tune marriage brings so much misery. It robs people of the emotional security of intimate belongingness. The whole spirit cries out against the injustice. Like Noah's dove, it has nowhere to place the sole of its feet.

This explains why marriage counseling has become of such vital importance both inside and outside the church. Happiness is very difficult to achieve without marital harmony. With many pastors this problem takes up most of their counseling time.

The demand to allay this misery rather parallels the cruel need for subsistent food and lodging of a century ago. Then William Booth and his Salvation Army ministered to the physically needy, and brilliantly used this service as a stepping-stone to Christ. I feel that we can do the same with this terribly obtrusive modern need to mend broken marriages.

This is no mere theoretical guess on my part. Because I was qualified as a clinical psychologist I was quickly drawn into this field of marriage counseling. My motive was purely to help people. But I quickly found that it paid unexpected evangelistic dividends. Many of those I counseled accepted Christ and joined the church.

Apparently two reasons were behind this. One of them was that the help I gave created a favorable rapport with me and therefore to the Christ I served. The other was that many of them quickly found that they needed a power beyond themselves to change sufficiently to make their marriages work.

It follows that just as General Booth's officers were required to become experts on social work, the present-day minister should be an expert on marriage problems. If he can become successful here, he will be sowing seeds for continuing successful evangelism too.

Apparently, as far as this drive to belong is concerned, marriage and family are not enough. Couples may be in wonderful rapport with one another and yet need to belong to other associations. Families may be very close and yet still experience the need for group relations to which they can intimately belong.

The realization of this hunger has brought about a most effective work of evangelism among young married couples. Reference has been made to this in a previous chapter, but here I want to consider it as more than a group relationship, but rather as something that satisfies the need to belong. The nucleus is a Sunday school class which is more like a club, with its own organization and officers. It is so integrated that its members look upon it as far more than a Sunday school class at which they are more or less passive recipients. It has become an entity in itself, capable of generating an emotional loyalty to it and its members. It is the focal point of their church activities, with the lesson period on Sundays, social gatherings during the week, coffees for the homemakers, projects for the good of the church and the community.

Some of these classes have their own worship services too. Actually what they have evolved is their own New Testament-type church within the local church, thus recapturing the tight fellowship of those times at this present period in history when the modern bigness of the church has well nigh destroyed it.

The way its evangelism works is like this: A member couple invites another couple with whom they are acquainted to a nonreligious gathering of the class: a party or a picnic or a bowling evening. The new couple is made particularly welcome and quickly gets to like the group. In no time at all, this inner drive to belong welds them into spiritual integration with the group. They find they have a built-in inclination to accept the group's religious goals before they even know about them. It becomes an easy step to graduate from the social functions to the religious activities. Then when the time is ripe they readily take the final step of personal committal to Christ.

My own experience has been that Christians won this way tend to stick far better than those who make decisions in response to preaching alone. Curiously enough, one of the big difficulties is not their conversion but their transition from the class to the church as a whole. For this reason ministers often criticize the whole approach. But it is not the small group which is at fault. It is the bigness of the church with its inability to produce any intimate feeling of belongingness. This is what people mean when they say they find a church is "cold." The problem may not be that the members are unfriendly. It is just that the situation is not such that the newcomer can readily belong. Failure to realize this vitiates a lot of the visitation evangelism which has become quite a replacement for "revival" or mass-meeting evangelism.

I can remember one "campaign" run very methodically by a professional at visitation evangelism. The members were carefully schooled on their approach, armed with cards to be signed by those seeking decisions. They were thrilled with their success. At the Easter ingathering nearly a hundred people were added to the church in one great mass occasion. But almost all of them quickly dropped out. This was perfectly predictable because there was no "belongingness integration."

It could have been much more effective if the evangelism procedure had been delayed and, instead, these people introduced a few at a time to small church groups, allowing them time and opportunity to belong. Then when they made their decision for Christ, they would have a ready-made spiritual home.

The Christian church is supposed to be a divine "family." In an ordinary family when a child is born, he is born into that family with parents and brothers and sisters who have had a vital interest in the whole process. He automatically belongs.

Much of present-day evangelism is of the foster-parent variety. The spiritual child is brought into the heavenly world by an outsider who then hands him over to a stranger who tries to bring him into a fellowship which is unfamiliar. Thus, at the start, the odds are against successful integration.

A spiritual child needs his spiritual parents for quite a while. Therefore the ideal situation for lasting evangelism is for it to occur within a tightly cohesive group.

This makes it tough for mass evangelistic efforts of the interdenominational variety. All of them are putting a great deal of time and effort into follow-up, but the results are depressing. It may be foster-parenthood at its best, but it's not the real thing.

This is not to decry the value of such large united efforts. They tend to put religion on the map in an area and make people God-conscious. This makes individual and group evangelism much easier, but it can never do the job of evangelism for the local church. Many are won by these efforts and some do last, and we can thank God for every one. But the real task is much more intimate.

It would appear that the present trend toward mergers will not favor evangelism. The larger the membership of a church, the bigger the proportion who are on the roll but who do not really belong. If we ever get to the stage where each town has just one community church, the number of active Christians in that town will sharply drop, and it will be much harder to win people in the first place. If the ecumenical superchurch is ever realized, the difficulty of achieving cohesive groups to which people identify and belong will be enormous.

I was very much intrigued by the methods used by Southern Baptists in their advance into California after World War II. They set up churches in homes and storefronts wherever they went. It all looked so undignified and "slum-like" in comparison with the lovely church edifices going up all around. But, on visiting a few, I was surprised to find that the membership was not at all composed merely of the poor and uneducated, but also of doctors, lawyers, businessmen, etc. These people wanted a place which was small enough for them to belong to. The success of the Southern Baptists, I think, stems from this. Many of these members are now not too happy that success has robbed them of this intimacy. Incidentally, the Southern Baptist rate of increase has leveled off somewhat since then. It figures.

I have made particular mention of the success with young married couples. Not all groups will have the same easy going. This is a naturally cohesive group because there is an excitement of common interest in this case that naturally draws them together. Without some powerful common factor, the going is really tough.

The important thing to realize for group evangelism is that the group is more than a collection of people. *They must be tied together by a common interest.* If this is not naturally present, it must be developed by group esprit de corps. There must be such group spirit and loyalty that the newcomers will feel the satisfying pull.

It also should be kept in mind that the interests which keep people together change or wither and die. A good example is the men's class, so popular and thriving fifty years ago, and now so very hard to promote. Now most men prefer mixed classes where they can go with their wives. Perhaps, more to the point, wives do not like their husbands going to functions like this without them.

At the turn of the century there was reason for segregation of the sexes. The standards of delicacy would have made

The Drive to Belong

frank discussion difficult otherwise. Now there is no longer any problem whatsoever. In any case, the mixed group is much better for the purposes of evangelism because it allows the couple to be won for Christ *together,* which is as it should be.

What has been said in this chapter about group evangelism through belongingness is especially relevant to youth. Isolation or not belonging is a fate which every young person fears worse than death. On the other hand, the chance to belong and participate in an active, satisfying group will draw him like a magnet.

I know this was a big factor in my own conversion. I disliked church and I resented preaching, but I became involved in a group of young people who were all out for Christ and thoroughly enjoying it. I wanted to belong to them in the most urgent way, and soon I wanted their Christ too.

If Christian young people want to win others, they are, therefore, wasting their time doing it on a "lone wolf" personal-evangelism basis. They need to build up a spiritual home *first* within the church. This is a group of young people vitally concerned with the developing of their own spiritual lives and with the Christian sense of mission. This should be broad enough to include social activities as well. In fact, it should be similar to the young married couples' group described earlier, except that it should be slanted to teenage experience and interests. If this is a real live cohesive group, conversions will be almost automatic.

I realize that the experienced alert pastor will have sensed an immediate danger in all this. It sounds as if I am encouraging "cliques," which are the bane of any church. Well, I guess I am.

Let us ask ourselves why "cliques" are so objectionable and yet so common. First, they are never objectionable to those who belong to them, only to those on the outside *who do not belong.* Second, they are common because people need them. So the answer is to encourage and promote such a variety of groups that everybody has a chance to belong. Of course, some never will. They are personality misfits who desperately need to belong but never can. But they present a special case, and the church cannot be organized on that basis. It has to be geared to the needs and abilities of the majority.

On the whole, there will not be much criticism about the group fellowships if they are openly promoted. Groups are regarded as cliques only when they slip in unawares and unwanted.

When the church is very large it becomes almost impossible to produce the degree of intimate belongingness that we so much long for. For true belongingness we need to know all the others intimately so that there can be the interaction of love. In many of our churches, members can pass each other on the street without any recognition that they are fellow church members. In such circumstances, members become mere statistics rather than people. This seems far from the New Testament concept of fellowship.

However, it is useless to try and stem the tide of bigness. With the expanding population, churches are bound to expand just as schools and universities do. The only answer seems to be that of fellowships within the church, possibly on an area basis. This way something can be built up which is small enough for people to cope with, that is, a group to which they can really belong.

The task of the pastor in this regard is becoming increasingly difficult, but somehow he has to succeed. Otherwise he will find himself presiding over what amounts to be a mere preaching station, and that is far from being a New Testament church.

If he can succeed he can almost certainly be guaranteed a stable membership with relatively few droputs. He can also be sure that it will be a soul-winning church because it will act like a magnet to appeal to this great human instinct to belong.

It was emphasized in the last chapter that people are hungrily seeking for a sense of mission in life. If, therefore, we can produce groups which satisfy the need to belong and which also have evangelism as a reason for their existence, we will have a combination which is hard to beat.

7

IDENTIFICATION

IN RECENT YEARS the psychology of reader identification has been given great attention, especially in the magazine field. It is important because it determines whether an article or story is going to be read. Most people start a piece with some sense of expectancy but drop it after a few paragraphs unless they are gripped by it in some way. This apparently depends on emotional identification.

In a good story with vivid, believable characterization, we seem to get into the skin of the protagonist. We feel we *are* him. As he struggles and suffers to achieve his goal, we sweat it out too. The tension is not released inside us until his crisis is successfully resolved. Until then we are reluctant to put the magazine down. This suspense is an important element in identification. We have to care what happens to the hero.

The modern magazine article extensively uses this fiction technique. Few people want to read straight information. Apparently the limit of the average reader for didactic material is no more than about three or four paragraphs. What the skillful writer does is to insert anecdotes at intervals. These attempt to keep the reader identified and, therefore, interested. The anecdotes show him *emotionally* how important the information is to him.

The same factor is at work in the case of the evangelistic

message, although the listener is not quite as free as the reader. The reader can toss the magazine aside at will, but the man in the pew is a captive until the end of the sermon, unless he is particularly uninhibited. However, he is not altogether defenseless. He can tune the preacher out and let his mind wander on more interesting matters. The point is that the preacher, if he wants to gain a decision and not waste the listener's time, must succeed in getting him to feel personally involved.

This is what people mean when they refer to a sermon as being "dry." It has failed to involve them. They are not identified in any way. On the other hand, a message is "gripping" if it has gripped *them,* if they have been emotionally pulled into it.

The use of the anecdote in religious messages is very old. There is an early case in the life of David when the prophet Nathan was seeking to bring conviction to the king about his adultery with Bathsheba and the murder of her husband. The prophet's story was about a rich shepherd who callously took a poor man's one ewe lamb to feed a guest. David was incensed at the injustice. His emotional involvement in the story made him a sitting duck for the prophet's aim.

Jesus used parables in the same way and this made His preaching tremendously popular. The common people could see themselves in the messages. So could the Pharisees: stories like the good Samaritan, the prodigal son, and the sower and the seed are simply unforgettable.

Actually, much of the thrust of the Bible comes from this approach. We see truth illustrated in the lives and deeds, the joys and heartaches of living men. The greatest message of all was not written or spoken. It was Jesus, the Word, the revelation of God *in a life.* A big factor in His impact upon our lives is that He is one with whom we can readily identify.

The most effective messages are those that capitalize on this effect, where straight exposition is very limited, and the truth becomes evident in the anecdote. This type of preaching requires laborious preparation, but it is worth it.

However, listener identification does more than keep him interested. It predisposes him in the direction of the derived change. If the anecdote is positive in that the protagonist makes the right decisions, the listener's empathy with that character will make him want to do the same. If the illustration is negative in that the central figure makes the wrong decision and suffers accordingly, the listener will be powerfully motivated not to make that error, since he has already vicariously suffered for it.

Identification can be aided or hindered by the preacher's manner of address. The old soapbox shouting bout sometimes appears to be effective because weaker personalities submit under the attack. But it is from without and, therefore, alien. There is no warm personal involvement, no motivation from within.

But even the cool, logical, reasoned approach can miss the boat if the listeners do not feel a person-to-person confrontation. I know a preacher who always says some very good things but I never feel he is talking to *me*. He seems to be addressing the air. You get the impression that he could give the same message with nobody there. He enunciates well, and he is quite fluent, but his tone in preaching is artificial, very different from his normal lively conversational voice. You accept what he says but you never feel involved.

Outside of the sermon situation, when someone has a message for us—no matter how urgent it is—he talks directly to us. Since we are used to this in person-to-person relationships, we will never get any real sense of message that *concerns* or *involves* us unless the same approach is used. The preacher needs to develop the skill of making each person of the congregation feel just as if he is being spoken to personally.

Evangelistic preaching is an attempt to "mass produce" personal persuasion. In this sense it is an illusion because

IDENTIFICATION

there are more persons there than the preacher and one other individual. Yet, for success, it has to *seem* to each person that this is all there are. This can happen only if the listener identifies with the message. If this happens, his preoccupation with it will tend to put all others out of the focus of his attention.

This will be possible only if the preacher cultivates the same illusion. That is, he must act and feel as if he is talking to only one person. Some speakers cultivate this by picking out one person in the audience and speaking directly to him as if nobody else were present. (Of course, when this device is used, the person singled out must be at the back or at someplace out of immediate focus so that the audience will be unaware of what the preacher is doing.) Some speakers use an empty chair and imagine someone is there and speak directly to him.

Whatever method is used to create the illusion, once it has been created, the speaker will find it impossible to use any unnatural or uncharacteristic platform-voice monotone or mannerism. On the positive side, the illusion will preserve all the variation, naturalness, color, and persuasiveness of conversation.

This does not mean that the *volume* has to be the same as that in conversation. Obviously, with a sizable audience it must be much louder; but when it is, it should be *amplified conversation,* not an entirely different breed of address. If there is no public address system, the speaker will have to speak at a volume greater than he usually does and this may destroy the illusion for him. For this reason, I personally advocate the use of a microphone even for small audiences because then the speaker can use his normal conversational level. The electronics will take care of the volume.

Another enemy to the feeling that each person is being spoken to personally is the use of clichés and religious jargon by the preacher. "Conservative" religion is especially guilty here. Those of us who have been brought up in it are so saturated with it that we forget that the outsider has little idea of what we are talking about. I refer to terms like "accepting Christ," "being saved," "the blood of Christ," "working in the Lord's vineyard." We know what we mean by such expressions, but others may not. Thus they cannot identify. We must say what we mean in nonthelogical English.

The use of King James English expressions such as those found in the version of the Bible that goes with his name are also bad. When we say such things as "if you believe not in Christ" instead or "if you don't believe in Christ," people get the impression that we are not really talking to them personally because in ordinary conversation we wouldn't dream of speaking like that.

This applies to prayers too. Others would think we were out of our minds if we spoke to them in the singsong voice, poetic and archaic language that we often belabor God with. The implication is that we do not believe that we are talking to a real person because nobody talks to real persons that way. If we want to persuade people that we believe God is real, then we must start to treat Him that way.

The preacher must never be a mere passive channel of the message. He has to be something akin to the biblical writers. God did not use them like impassive typewriters. The message is percolated through their own individual personalities retaining all the color and warmth of their personal idiosyncracies.

With the preacher, the message comes from God through the minister like milk comes from grass through the cow. The cow eats the grass which becomes part of its total bodily processes and from that comes the milk. "Truth through personality," Phillips Brooks called it. Anything less is artificial.

The message with which we can identify is that which the preacher is *himself experiencing*. In this sense the sermon

IDENTIFICATION

is essentially a witness. The witness is far more than the evangelist testifying as to how he was "saved." This soon becomes old hat. It goes beyond the telling of warm, homely incidents from the preacher's own life, although they can help. It is the feeling that is given that the minister is experiencing the God that he is talking about.

That is not subject to techniques. It cannot be counterfeited or cooked up. There is no shortcut. There is no alternative to the personal awareness of an experienced God.

There is no area in life where truth tells more transparently than in religion. We can't get away with any attempt to preach the gospel message from the outside in any theoretical way. It is utterly useless to argue: "Well, I haven't experienced all this myself, but it is in the Word of God, so I can preach it anyway." It has to come from the inside. Everything else sounds hollow.

It isn't that people expect us to be perfect. It is just that when we speak of a God who can transform, they expect to see Him in action in our lives. If people are living in the same town with a minister who is arrogant, negative, argumentative, domineering and spiteful, they will not be impressed by his statements that God can "break every chain."

This doesn't mean that we must wait until we are perfect before we can preach, but it does mean that we must be *in the process* of experiencing God's power before we can proclaim it. There is nothing like reality to give the impression of reality. In life-and-death matters like this, people aren't interested in theory!

Although the kind of identification that produces life-changing action can come through the sermon, many now question whether the sermon is the most effective way. They think that dialogue or discussion is more effective.

Dialogue is not new. Socrates used it with devasting effectiveness. His method was to ask searching questions. Constant probing made many false views untenable. But Socrates' intention was not to be destructive. He simply was after truth on a secure foundation. Every answer had to come from the disciples' own mind. He himself was unavoidably identified with it from the start.

Some years ago an interesting experiment was carried out to determine the relative effectiveness of group discussion as against straight exhortation. The aim was to bring about more hygienic and sanitary practices in a slum area. In one group, the participants were merely urged by a speaker to makes the changes. The other comparable group discussed the proposed changes among themselves without any outside speaker. The second group made more of the desired changes than the first group, and the results were more permanent.

The explanation seems to be that in the group discussion the women identified themselves with their own decisions. In carrying them out, they were not obeying the will of others. They were doing what they had decided to do and wanted to do.

The effectiveness of group discussion in the learning process has long been recognized by education experts. The psychology behind it is the same: motivation through identification. But in evangelism it is largely untried.

The best way to use identification through group discussion is in meetings in homes. Such groups should be carefully planned so that most of those present are committed Christians. This will guarantee the group "set" toward the Christian faith. But this should never be a mere gimmick in which everything is cut and dried, with the method merely a technique to trick the unconverted. Topics or Bible studies used should be sufficiently open in that real answers are wanted. The evangelism comes in as a slant on whatever issues are involved. No matter what the problem is, the possibility of a life transformed in conversion by God is always relevant.

But identification can come through action too. Forty years

IDENTIFICATION

ago Hugh Redwood got started on his impact-laden career as a Christian journalist by an encounter with the Salvation Army in an emergency in the slums of London. His participation in those rescue operations so moved him emotionally that he became identified with it. This involvement in just one aspect of the great work of redemption identified him with the total program of Christ. He was never the same after that.

Earlier in this book, reference is made to the involvement in groups, using a person's natural drive to belong. Identification is simply a further step. Thus, both drives can work together.

The secret seems to be to get people involved. Many a man owes his Christian faith to his participation in a working bee at the church. People get drawn in through scouts, youth programs, social work, special drives. Some are won through financial investment. Whether it is effort or time or money, they become involved. Identification is an easy step from there, and from thence to identification with Christ.

These new approaches to identification do not mean that preaching has to be abandoned. Preaching, group discussions, and group action are by no means mutually exclusive. They can all be used.

If the psychology of identification has relevance to the problem of winning a person initially, it is even more effective in conserving him after he is won. It welds the newly identified person, reversing the tendency to drift. It will be in line with his psychological needs for him to remain and, even more significant, to remain active.

8
RAPPORT

Rapport is the congenial emotional atmosphere between people which eases communication and increases suggestibility. On the negative side it is the feeling between people which neutralizes contrasuggestion and negativeness.

Our first contact with a person, whether individually or in a crowd, arouses an instinct to protect ourselves. He may not harm us physically but he could wound our sensitive egos, he could belittle us, he could cause us to change, he could penetrate our guard against suggestion, he could prove or appear superior to us, he could affect our status with others. Although some of these things could be highly desirable in the long run, they are decidedly unpleasant to the personality and arouse fear and resentment.

Psychologically, this wall that we set up between ourselves and the impact of other personalities is tied up with the ego drive described earlier in this book. The full force of the self is turned outward toward the environment of people and things, searching for fulfillment, satisfaction, and recognition. But others are involved in this same pursuit, and we know well enough that they may win out in the struggle for some of the ego prizes, or they may rob us of some of the ego rewards we have already acquired. Thus every new person we meet is a potential enemy or possible threat. This may make no rhyme or reason intellectually, but it makes sense emotionally, and that is the decisive factor.

Rapport

It follows that to gain the rapport necessary to break down this barrier we have to reassure the ego somehow. The person we want to approach must be made to feel emotionally that not only has he nothing to fear, but that the encounter promises further fulfillment for him.

This protective instinct problem shows itself as an initial coldness. It is a well-known difficulty for social gatherings. Nobody enjoys himself until the "ice is broken." The hostess tries to produce rapport by warm introductions, lighthearted banter, by "mixing" games and, in some circles, by alcohol. Alcohol tends to break down any inhibition and, therefore, turns out to be quite effective, so it is said. However, it is not recommended for evangelistic work!

Introductions do not help unless they make the guest feel important. The clever hostess frames them in such a way that interest is aroused on the part of the other guests. Since we like people to be interested in us, the new encounter immediately becomes an ego-satisfying experience, and the resistance evaporates.

The effect of the "mixing" process is to make the guest feel that he belongs. Until that happens it may seem to him that he is unwanted or unimportant. His integration into the group will appear to him as an achievement, a conquest, and this will bring the corresponding emotional glow: rapport.

It follows that the "mixing" activity must be such that it will readily involve all the guests. If it is something that some cannot take part in, or that they will be too shy or timid to try, then there will be a feeling of isolation and rejection. Lack of careful planning here can easily make the rapport problem infinitely worse.

Churches face the problem with regard to visitors, who may be consciously, or unconsciously, afraid for two reasons. They may fear that they may not be accepted, that they may not belong, or they may be scared that they will be drawn into something that they don't want. In either case there is resistance. If it is not broken down they will project and accuse the church of being "cold" and "not friendly."

This matter of whether a church is cold or friendly is a very relative thing. I can remember in one week getting two entirely contradictory reports about a church. One visitor who had attended a certain service wrote later in glowing terms that in all his years of travel he had never been made to feel so much at home. Yet, another man, who was present at that same service, said he had found people so disinterested and cold that he would never go there again!

The rather abusive attitude of the second man gave him away as a most insecure person. This is often the case with those who complain of coldness; they do not put themselves out to be friendly. If they did, it would be most unlikely that they would be rejected. Instead, they are passive, expecting the initiative to be all on the other side, as might occur with visiting royalty!

It is a most unfortunate attitude, nevertheless we cannot wash our hands of it. It may be pandering to egotism, but if we are going to win the visitor we will have to make him feel like royalty. Whatever it takes to break down that wall, that is what we have to do. Otherwise we will never reach him with the gospel.

This initial impression may be critical for evangelism because contact through the casual visit to the church may be the only chance we will get. Nowadays churches are aware of the danger. They have welcoming committees at the door who may tag the visitor so that the congregation will be alerted to the need and know to whom to talk. Then there is always the warm public welcome in the service. Often this is followed up later by visits to the home of the visitor, telephone calls, and invitations to social occasions.

Generally this has to be organized or it will become nobody's job, but the organization itself can be a danger. It can

Rapport

give the impression to the visitor that he is only a part of a planned program, a "contact," and that all this is being put on, that the church thinks of him as a statistic rather than wanting him as a person. The only way to avoid this is for everybody to be sincere, not saying anything unless it is really meant.

Of course, welcoming can go too far. One visitor once complained to me that his family had been visited by no less than six enthusiastic laymen in one week!

With the evangelistic purpose, whether in a meeting or in the personal confrontation, the danger of emotional resistance is greatly increased because the setup acts as an automatic warning that a siege on the personality is about to begin.

Most happily unconverted people avoid the danger altogether by staying clear of evangelistic meetings, which makes sense from their point of view. They don't want to change, so why go somewhere where someone is going to try to convert them?

For this reason, meetings that are advertised as "evangelistic" tend to defeat their own purpose. Christians, unless they feel a sense of obligation to swell the crowd, stay away because the message is not for them. The unconverted stays away because he knows he will be singled out and become a target.

It makes better sense to arrange meetings to be more general, where the messages are directed to everybody, Christian and non-Christian. The important thing is to let God speak to whom He wants and not define His audience for Him. Slanting what is said to the unconverted is not difficult. It doesn't necessitate the whole sermon. Experience shows that this is just as effective evangelism as zeroing in on the unbeliever for a whole service. In any case, it does a lot to increase rapport.

The term *revival*, which has had quite an honored history

in evangelism, now carries negative public relations. In many people's minds it suggests hot-gospeler antics and a trap to catch the unwary when he is emotionally off guard.

Headings like "Crusade for Christ," "Deeper-Life Mission" and "Abundant-Living Drive" tend to increase rapport because they promise something for all of us without singling any of us out.

The advertising of the preacher himself may also build up resistance if it is not intelligently planned. One of the worst things to do is to play up the evangelist's success as a soul-winner in terms of numbers. Imagine yourself as a non-Christian being invited to listen to a preacher who has won "2,437 souls" in five years. The inference is that he now wants you in his bag of trophies. There is nothing more demeaning to the ego than to be just another statistic. If you do go to hear him you are going to have all the barriers up. It is going to be a personal satisfaction to you to be able to resist such a champion!

In planning promotion for a crusade it is not a bad idea to put yourself in the average non-Christian's place. You are quite happy as you are and you don't want to change unless it is your own idea. If we gear our advertising to meet that ego situation we will be far less likely to defeat our own purposes as we often do now.

It should not be imagined that rapport is a difficulty only for those on the receiving end. The preacher, or evangelist himself, has a problem. We say he has to "warm up." At the start, he may be unsure of himself and his effectiveness to get his message over, especially if the congregation is new to him. As he proceeds, and as he feels his audience responding, he gains confidence and can really put his heart into it.

Actually, there is a "feedback" effect. When the preacher feels that his audience is "with him," he relaxes and induces his increased confidence to the people, who correspondingly "warm up" to him.

Rapport

The biggest problem in gaining rapport with an audience is the initial ego resistance. They recognize that here is a speaker who is aiming to persuade them and thus win a personality victory over them. In other words, there is an ego war. Unless the speaker succeeds in neutralizing this, he has had it.

Curiously enough, humor and especially laughter are most effective in getting an audience into a receptive mood. It is even more effective if the joke is of the belittling variety and used by the speaker against himself. In the first uneasy and tense moments of an address, even a trifling misadventure about himself that the speaker relates may be greeted with great hilarity.

There is good psychological reason for this. As has been pointed out, the speaker-audience situation presents an ego threat. To make up for this we want to feel good in comparison with the speaker. Therefore, when he tells a belittling joke on himself we look better in comparison, and the nervous tension is released by laughter.

This is why there are so many jokes on those in authority, professors, teachers, statesmen. They are funny because they satisfyingly decrease the ego gap between us and them.

But quite apart from laughter, a speaker can lessen ego resistance by readily admitting his own limitations. None can claim to have achieved perfection anyway. With the apostle Paul, we merely "follow after."

On the other hand, the evangelist can cut his throat rapportwise by talking favorably about himself. Since he too has an ego stake here, this won't be easy. Inevitably there will be internal pressures to gild the lily in his favor. He will find himself doing quite irrelevant name-dropping of the great and the famous whose paths he has crossed, or alluding in only near-context to his achievements or honors. Personal references can add a lot to any message, but they should be pruned very carefully for egotistical accretions.

Audience rapport can be helped a great deal by not using the "you" approach. It is much better to say "we," thus associating oneself with the congregation. Preaching at people gives the impression that the speaker considers himself to be in a superior class.

However, there is a "we" usage which is much worse than the "you" address, and that is the editorial or royal "we." This is when the preacher says "It is our opinion" when he means "It is my opinion." Fortunately, this affectation has now almost totally disappeared.

Tone of voice, such as soapbox-style oratory, can also hinder rapport. People like to feel that the preacher respects their personalities enough not to shout at them. As mentioned earlier, the best tone seems to be that kind of conversational approach where the audience feels that the preacher is taking them into his confidence. Abuse, of course, just defeats its own purpose.

Perhaps the goal of a good atmosphere can be summed up by saying that the preacher has to succeed in getting the audience to like him as a person. I know that there have been giants in the past like Elijah and John the Baptist who didn't need to worry about rapport, and even got away with abusing their audiences. If the modern evangelist can aspire to that degree of greatness he might get away with it, too but—

Much of the same kind of principle applies to personal evangelism. But here, even greater care is necessary. A person in an audience feels himself protected somewhat by the anonymity of being one with a crowd, but in the person-to-person approach there is nowhere to hide. Consequently the seeker may feel most insecure, and this will make him unnecessarily negative.

The usual reaction to this fear is to counter the evangelist with argument and even hostility. If he is experienced at all it will be an easy matter to demolish the objections, but this is the worst thing to do. It will make the non-Christian lose face and vastly increase his ego resistance to the message. Someone has put it this way: "'You may win your argument but you'll lose your man."

The understanding Christian will want to let the other person down lightly. Almost every point of view has an element of truth in it, and this provides a good starting point. It pays to look for this and recognize it, thus making the contact feel that he has made a contribution. Head-on collisions should be avoided. The secret is to elicit the truth from the man rather than appear to be imposing this upon him. There is no place for cleverness or a smart-aleck attitude in personal evangelism.

Dogmatism is a deadly enemy of rapport. Actually, the more concerned the Christian is, the more likely he will be tempted to be dogmatic. Many excuse themselves on this score by saying they are being "true" to an infallible Bible, but they should keep in mind that there is a great deal of difference between an infallible Bible and an infallible *interpretation* of the Bible.

In any case, it is quite possible to be thoroughly convinced of a point of view without being dogmatic. In many cases the dogmatic emphasis is a cover-up for actual uncertainty.

Modern salesmanship has emphasized the need to consider the prospect as a person and to be interested in him as a person rather than as merely a sale. Having a salesman advise against a sale is now not unusual. This gives the impression to the person approached that he is not a potential victim of an onslaught but a friend being helped. The difference in rapport is enormous.

The statistical approach is a great enemy here. It is an offense against the dignity of man to be processed like cattle. Nobody wants to be a mere cipher among fifty people won at a revival. Every man is a person so valuable that Christ died for him. This means that he must be treated with respect and love. He must be made to feel that the personal evangelist is interested in him as a whole, real person and not just in his "immortal soul."

The most effective personal evangelists are those whose every action and word underlie their respect for the personalities of others. These gospel heralds never talk down to people, because they do not feel themselves superior. They know that although their faith is steadily changing them toward the image of Christ, it has not made angels out of them. Neither has it given them infallibility in opinion. They are humble people, so grateful for what Christ has done for them that they want to share it with others.

They are the kind of people that everybody refers to as "nice." They are men of deep conviction yet their approach is quiet, humble, unassuming. You can't help liking them, and that is a big step toward wanting the Saviour they represent.

9
BACKGROUND RAPPORT

BESIDES THE MORE DIRECT TYPE of rapport discussed in the previous chapter there is also a background rapport that needs to be taken into account. This is the psychology behind what is popularly known as "public relations." It is the favorable atmosphere created in the community which predisposes its members toward the goals of the group concerned.

This favorable rapport is vital for evangelism for two reasons. It largely determines whether there will be any contacts in the first place, and, second, it affects the effectiveness of the message when it is heard.

The problem of getting contacts is becoming more difficult all the time because people do not drift into services and meetings the way they used to do. This is true of all meetings, not just the religious type. In less busy days, and especially before television and radio, the religious, political, and cultural meetings were a prime source of entertainment, or at least something to do. Now life is full of entertaining interests, in comparison with which most meetings rate very poorly indeed.

We emphasize now that every meeting has to be promoted; that is, we must build up such artificial interest so that people will be motivated to come.

This is certainly true. Merely to announce a meeting, either verbally or in the papers, is to doom it to failure. Even when such a world-renowned figure as Billy Graham comes to town, the announcement of this fact is not enough. The public relations men go to work long before. They not only promote but seek to gain commitments by people to be present at the meetings.

Most churches do not have this prestige or these resources, so they have to motivate people in other ways. Usually this is by personal invitation, but this is not effective unless there already exists a predisposition toward the church and its work on the part of the public as a whole.

In any community a considerable number of people are kindly disposed toward religion but are not yet motivated to do any thing about it. However, their interest may be sufficient to bring them to church occasionaly if that interest can be triggered by some small emotional predisposition toward the church. This can be accomplished by background rapport.

However, getting them to church or the meeting is only the start. Attendance is not the goal. What we are after is committal to Christ. Therefore, we not only want people to be present when the gospel is proclaimed, we want them to be in such a frame of mind that they are favorably oriented toward making this decision. This can be accomplished by good public relations. Otherwise they will be "cold."

Background rapport is essentially an emotional atmosphere, but this cannot exist in vacua. There has to be a medium for it, and this comes from awareness. Awareness itself is neutral, and it can be the basis of either positive or negative feeling, but no feeling is possible without it. In other words, unless the community knows that the church exists, there can be no reaction of any kind.

This awareness is so imporatnt to public relations that many claim no publicity can ever be bad, that even bad publicity is good because it makes people aware of you, who otherwise would not be. Many an evangelist has been incensed at an attack on him in the press, only to find that it was the best thing that could have happened. It aroused people's interest enough to bring them out to see for themselves. Certainly this has proved true on book sales. The royal road to bestsellerdom was to get the book banned in Boston.

Advertising is therefore essential if the church or the crusade is to be put on the map. However, advertising has to be discriminating or it may be a waste of money. A two-line notice in the church advertisement page is obviously not going to accomplish much. In this connection, advertising should be constantly checked for effectiveness. It also should be venturesome, using initiative and imagination to explore new avenues of approach.

But the best advertising is *news*. Whenever the church or a member does something that is worthwhile, someone should make sure it gets into the local news channels. When a speaker or evangelist comes to town, he should be featured. The usual publicity sheets with their accumulation of superlatives do not help too much. The public is immune to that. It is the human-interest element that gets through. An interview by a good and sympathetic reporter will get this in the paper, but someone in the church or group should make a careful study first and then feed the reporter with choice tidbits. Without this the newsman is not likely to be interested in the first place.

Actually, although awareness is essential to rapport, it does not need to *precede* it. It can be part of the same process. Indeed, it is better this way. There can be a steady buildup of public relations in which the church can become known and liked at the same time.

This goal can be achieved through the development of image. Unfortunately, one of the biggest obstacles to evangelism that we have, especially with young people, is unfavorable image. We seem to have inherited a sorry picture from Puritanism. To many, the Christian faith is deprivation, exile from life, moralism, and often bigotry and fanaticism.

The early church did not project this image. Actually, Jesus was accused of enjoying life too much (Mt 11:19). He Himself emphasized that He had come to bring life and that more abundantly (Jn 10:10). He was seldom negative. His whole approach was attractive, positive.

The big problem of Puritanism was that it identified sin with enjoyment, a marriage that was neither made in heaven nor on earth. Even now "worldliness" is often made to be synonymous with "amusements," leading to dreary, damaging debates as to whether it is right for a Christian to play football, watch television, dance, etc., thus sidetracking the New Testament attack on worldliness as the obsession with any material things that impair one's relationship with God.

Of course there will always be activities that will rightly be considered as harmful; but if a good image is to be raised, it must be made clear that the attack against them is on the basis that these lessen or destroy enjoyment in living and not because there is anything wrong with fun itself.

In making these attacks it should first be critically determined that the activity is indeed wrong and forbidden by Scripture and not a mere cultural carry-over from a previous generation.

In any case, the positive approach is far better. If we emphasize the joys of a deeper life with Christ, and people find this experience, the shady things in their lives will be burned out by inner spiritual fire. This way there is no danger of incidental, bad-image development.

I feel, too, that churches should be very wary about involvement in political or public campaigns which are in fafor of restricting the behavior of the citizens, even when it is felt to be in their own best interest. It is the church's job to redeem men, not to reform them. This kind of activity can give such a snobbish image that evangelism will be seriously hindered. Jesus warned us against the folly of straining at a gnat and swallowing a camel (Mt 23:24). What have we gained if we cut off an hour or two of an unbeliever's drinking time if in the process we have soured hundreds against Christ?

Obviously we do have a responsibility to take action against social evils; but, except in cases where the whole community recognizes the problem to be an evil, it is better that such intervention be by Christians as private citizens rather than by the church. Otherwise we will give the impression that the church is trying to impress its religious ideas on the rest of the community whether they want them or not.

But in areas where there is unanimity, such as carelessness causing traffic injury, juvenile delinquency, illiteracy, and human distress, the church can well be in the vanguard of action and, in so doing, create an admirable public image.

The question resolves itself into being one of strategy. In view of our dual goals of evangelism and community betterment, is it better for the church or the church member to take action?

It has been said that in most Muslim countries the only type of mission that has succeeded in making a breakthrough is the medical mission. The alleviation of physical pain creates such a favorable rapport that the barrier of fanaticism is broken and the heart becomes open to the gospel.

This is a universal principle. In American pastorates I have always been careful not only to personally put great attention on hospital visitation, but also to arrange for a strong program of deaconesses and elders doing the same. I have noted over the years that a high proportion of those visited became Christians, which was a direct result, but there was also the indirect dividend that the news of this work got around, and the community became kindly disposed toward the church that sponsored it.

Actually, it helps tremendously if the minister of a church

is prominent in his community in efforts for social betterment such as Community Fund, youth work, charitable organizations, major health programs (such as Cancer Fund). It is even better if it becomes well known that his church members are active too.

Then there are special things that a church can do with telling effect. In some country places I have seen telephone directories put out as a complimentary services to the town by the Mormons. It is nice to occasionally see a little park, or a bus shelter, or a playground given to the community by a church. Some churches create similar rapport by making their own building facilities available for the public good.

This kind of involvement preaches loud that the church cares for the community as such and for the members of the community as people, rather than merely as "souls" to be saved. In this way the church becomes known as part of the community, which dissolves the distaste with which people always view exclusiveness. When any group isolates itself from its community, it gives the impression of pharisaism, that it is too good to mix with the common people. This natually offends the egos of the outsiders and builds up resentment and a most unfavorable image.

At first sight this seems to put us on the spot in view of the scriptural command to "come out from among them, and be ye separate" (2 Co 6:17). But this is cleared up by what follows: "Touch not the unclean thing." We are to be in the world but not of it. Jesus Himself apparently lived quite an active social life. He certainly did not believe that mixing with people in community life implied the condoning of any of their evil practices. We should separate ourselves from evil in that we do not participate in wrongdoing, but we must not separate ourselves from people. Otherwise there is no witness.

The image of Billy Graham has succeeded nicely in making this distinction. His voice has been loud and clear against evil, and his own life has been impeccable. Yet there is nothing monastic or exclusive about him. He is very much a part of the life of his country. You don't see him heading a protest march, yet his personal stand against any social injustice is crystal clear. His image, as a result, is distinctly sympathetic and favorable. Perhaps this is why so many non-Christians go to hear him, already half anticipating to accept Christ even before they hear him.

When this is compared with some of our narrow, exclusive, critical, and anticommunity churches, it is easy to see why the outreach of such churches is so limited. Their image is appalling.

Where this exclusiveness also is directed against other Christian groups the image becomes quite disgraceful. The group acting in this way may be doing so in good conscience or on the basis of their interpretation of Scripture, but this doesn't change things. Even outsiders *know* this behavior is wrong, and no amount of hairsplitting theology will change that conviction. Many of them also know what Jesus said about this kind of thing: "And John answered him, saying, Master, we saw one casting out devils in thy name, and he followeth not us: and we forbad him, because he followeth not us. But Jesus said, Forbid him not: for there is no man which shall do a miracle in my name, that can lightly speak evil of me. For he that is not against us is on our part" (Mk 9:38-40).

This matter of fraternizing with other churches becomes quite a problem in view of the fact that so many of them may be ineffective. Cooperation with them may appear to the busy pastor as a waste of time. As far as actual concrete accomplishments are concerned, this may well be true; but there is more to it than that. This kind of brotherliness is an investment in good public relations.

Actually the psychology of good commnuity rapport turns out to be little more than good Christianity. If the church is as Christian as its Master and loves "the other sheep which are not of this fold" as He does, then the public relations will be all that could be desired in predisposing people toward His gospel.

10

THE POWER OF GUILT

THE THEORIES of Sigmund Freud have long since become outmoded as unscientific, oversimplified, and inadequate, yet one of his emphases is as strong as ever: the power of guilt.

No degree of sophistication seems to succeed in avoiding guilt. If the wrongdoer has such a hardened conscience that he does not "feel guilty," his insides will be eaten away by unconscious guilt, which is infinitely more dangerous.

Every person has feelings about what he ought to do and what he ought not to do. This sense of moral obligation plus universal failure to live up to it bring guilt.

To account for the subjectivity about moral obligation, Kant saw a difference between form and content. By "form" he meant capacity to feel moral obligation. By "content" he meant *what* a person feels obliged to do.

For instance, take a Christian's attitude toward a war in which his country is involved. He feels that as a citizen he is necesarily morally involved, that is the form. But he may feel impelled to fight on behalf of his country, or he may be convinced he must be a conscientious objector; this is the content. The form is the same for everyone. The content varies from person to person.

Guilt is quite independent of the content of moral obligation. If a man feels he ought to go to war and does not, he may experience just as sharp a sense of guilt as a man who feels he should not participate in military action and yet does.

Theologians draw a distinction between objective guilt and subjective guilt. Objective guilt is the guilt a man has in the eyes of God whether he feels guilty or not. It corresponds to a "guilty" verdict in a human court of law. Once it is pronounced, it is totally unaffected by the convicted person's own mental state.

The Christian evangelist has a deep responsibility to minister to this need. Reconciliation with God is at the very heart of the Christian gospel. But it is not the kind of guilt which is being dealt with in this chapter. We are concerned here with the impact of psychological or subjective guilt.

Subjective guilt is how a person *feels* about his own sin. It generally has an objective basis, but not always so. It is not unusual to find a person feeling guilty quite unnecessarily, such as when a man is tortured by guilt for causing an accident which turns out to be not his fault at all.

Subjective or psychological guilt may be either conscious or unconscious; that is, we may be aware of it or we may not. As mentioned earlier, unconscious guilt may be by far the most devasting kind. But both types generate powerful reactions to bring about the removal of guilt.

The capacity to feel guilt depends a great deal upon our physical and nervous state. Our degree of fulfillment of moral obligation is never yes or no. It is a wide spectrum which varies from our reaction to the most minuscule matters to the most vital crises. Our score is never zero and never 100 percent.

The normal person learns to live with his imperfections. There is always an area in which he is falling short, but he develops a sense of proportion about his corresponding feeling of guilt. For instance, he may be aware that he owes someone a letter but unless there is some urgency about it, he doesn't lose much sleep about it. But if he gives way to illicit passion he may be torn apart with grief.

Apparently this abilty to react with a sense of balance and

The Power of Guilt

proportion takes a great deal of mental energy. For when we get run down or suffer nervous debility we lose this. We find ourselves giving way to guilt about the tiniest and most insignificant things. The same tendency occurs when we are tired or ill. In the abnormal state, the sense of guilt may become acute that the sufferer is driven to suicide.

One curious aspect of the guilt of the mentally disturbed or nervously ill person (and some normal people) is the obsession with "the unforgiveable sin." Sometimes the patient has no idea what this unpardonable sin is; nevertheless, he is sure he has committed it.

Often it is associated with "blasphemy against the Holy Ghost" (Mt 12:31, etc.). Most commentators explain this as being the final rejection of the Holy Spirit's invitation to salvation rather than anything as superficial as a casual swear word involving God's name. Yet, I have known of people who are tortured with a compulsion to "curse" the Holy Spirit, and when they have done so, they go through the terrors of the damned.

This heightened sensitivity to guilt when it occurs is also generally characterized by an obsession with technicalities. One man I know of became terribly worried, years after his baptism, which was by immersion, because the top of his head hadn't gone under the water. Another was eaten up inside because he hadn't sold all his goods and given them to the poor as Christ instructed the rich young ruler to do. These sufferers seem especially prone to get hung up on the literal fulfillment of verses in the Bible.

In these cases of abnormal guilt, the cure, of course, involves more than any words or assurances that the evangelist can give. It is more a symptom of his nervous or psychiatric illness. Ridiculing his feelings of guilt will not help; neither will trying to explain them away logically. Exhortations to "pull himself together" or "snap out of it" are equally futile.

If he is sick, he needs treatment, medically or psychiatrically; often both.

However, although the treatment of symptoms alone is a poor way to cure a disease, such treatment is, nevertheless, important. The physician who gives injections to cure the basic problem simultaneously treats the lesions caused by the disease. For this reason the Christian doctrine of the forgiveness of sins can give tremendous relief.

Once again the relevance of the New Testament is most evident. Christ apparently often associated the forgiveness of sins with His healing work. His preaching encouraged people to seek this grace. The apostolic preaching made it an essential part of the evangelistic message.

One of the most telling verses in the Bible is 1 John 1:7, "The blood of Jesus Christ [God's] Son cleanseth us from all sin." As a clinical psychologist, I have used this again and again on guilt-ridden souls, and as it has sunk in, I have been greatly impressed by the tremendous surge of relief that has come over the sufferer.

There is no doubt that today's preacher of the gospel can make a most significant contribution to the alleviation of human suffering if the doctrine of the forgiveness of sins is given sufficient emphasis. The evangelist can be dead sure that even in the smallest congregation there will be people whose souls are being eroded by pernicious guilt. In many cases they are ashamed to talk about it to others and, therefore, can only be reached by God Himself. This kind of therapy is a significant by-product of the Christian gospel.

However, the presence of this irritated sense of guilt and the frantic drive for its removal also provide strong motivation toward conversion, if the evangelist slants his message toward it. But to be effective, this aspect must be *spelled out*. Generally people do not themselves work out such implications, no matter how great their need. The preacher must *specifically* make the application.

THE POWER OF GUILT

At first it would seem that all the sufferer needs is to be told of the availability of God's forgiveness. But actually, the problem is much deeper. What he needs is emotional awareness of forgiveness. The message cannot be merely intellectual or logical; it has to be a *suffering* forgiveness. It has to appear costly and there must be an element of punishment.

When I say *must*, I'm not referring to logical or theological necessity, but psychological need. It used to be the fashion among some theologians to belittle this element in the doctrine of the atonement, but this is shortsighted. The continual testimony of the historic church to sacrificial and penal elements in salvation was apparently an instinctive reference to needs much deeper than the mind alone.

It is very noticeable that the Bible portrays God as a suffering God, and Christ as a suffering Messiah. The crucifixion has always been at the heart of the gospel. So has been the doctrine of redemption: the efforts of a brokenhearted God seeking to rescue the lost. Preaching which highlights this fact brings the message of forgiveness to the existential level of the soul. Forgiveness is emotionally accepted only when the suffering soul coalesces with the suffering Spirit of God.

Objective theories of the atonement (in which God accomplishes something by the death of Christ and on the basis of which He can forgive) are psychologically much more satisfying than subjective theories (in which atonement is thought of as merely the subjective change in the believer moved to it by his sympathy with Christ's sufferings). Paul, of course, placed heavy emphasis on the cross as a penalty borne by Christ to appease the wrath of God. The reference by Jesus to His death as a ransom shows that His thinking contained the same elements. Because Christ did not always spell out the basis of forgiveness it must not be taken to imply that there was no objective basis there.

This book is not the place to discuss the theological debate on the penal issues on atonement. The purpose here is purely psychological and practical. What I am saying is that forgiveness without punishment is not red-blooded enough to reach deep enough into man's experiential need. When the Bible says that "the blood of Christ" cleanses us from sin rather than merely that God cleanses, it is aiming at that existential level.

The psychological basis for this need is the innate relationship which the mind recognizes between guilt and punishment. This is most dramatically illustrated in the functional diseases (the ailments which have no known physical cause), where the mind, in recognizing the unconscious desire for punishment to atone for guilt, may cripple bodily functions, bringing about pain, paralysis, blindness, etc. There is reason to believe that people may be driven to have accidents for the same reason.

The acceptance of forgiveness is, therefore, unlikely to be anything more than superficial unless the seeker is convinced that his sin has been punished, and the New Testament message—that the sin has been punished in Christ—meets that need.

This feeling of guilt can bring about another curious side effect. It may drive the unconscious mind to destroy religious belief in a kind of wishful thinking. Take the following illustration.

A young university student was obviously seeking, yet he seemed bedeviled by intellectual doubts. However, when one was explained to him, he simply raised another in tedious succession. In a stab in the dark the counselor suddenly asked: "You have a sexual problem, don't you?" The youth admitted it. Later he gave up the sin and accepted forgiveness. When he did, his intellectual problems evaporated without further discussion.

It is possible that some atheism may be similar wishful

thinking. The guilty soul hopes to goodness that there is no God because, if there is, he is in trouble.

A word of caution is necessary here. Not all intellectual doubt stems from this source by any means. Much of it is just what appears to be on the surface: an honest attempt to solve problems which are certainly objective enough in their own right.

But what of those who apparently feel no conscious guilt? As has been shown above, this does not mean that no guilt exists. Indeed, it is unconscious. Then it is as dangerous psychologically as an undetected cancer is physically. The preacher can do a great service by bringing it to the surface. In so doing he will also be arousing a powerful drive toward the acceptance of the gospel message of forgiveness.

Latent guilt cannot be brought out in general terms. Reference to sin in general is too vague and undefined to bring any response. It is true, of course, that the basic problem is the sinful state, or attitude, but this can never be meaningful unless it is first spotlighted by something more specific.

Billy Graham is particularly skillful in dealing with this problem. When he is speaking to young people he may pinpoint sexual sins and the damage they do. When he talks to a group of women he may refer to gossip or nagging, and how it sours human relationships. When he preaches to husbands he may hit at neglect and self-centeredness and how they dry up marital love. When talking to businessmen he may attack dishonesty or exploitation of employees, and how it poisons society.

When the nail is hit on the head with regard to one particular sin, attention is drawn to the sick state of the whole spiritual organism. Guilt is made conscious, and the pain it causes calls urgently for release. The great numbers who respond to Billy Graham's appeal are evidence of just how potent this approach can be.

However, it is extremely important that the sins referred to should be real and significant. They must be of such a nature that without question the listener will recognize the wrongness. That seems to be determined by two factors: Is the sin specifically referred to in the Bible, and does it have an obvious evil effect upon the welfare and happiness of others?

There is no room for preacher's personal fads. The message appears to be trifling and ridiculous when the attack is leveled on television-watching, miniskirts, hairdos, cosmetics, etc. Under the stress of great emotion, guilt can be induced on anything; but when the circumstances are removed, the victim feels like a fool and the permanent effect is negative.

In any case, the appeal to guilt should be used sparingly. Otherwise the overall effect will be negative and unattractive. People soon become case-hardened. The Christian gospel does not zero in on sin but on Christ. The doctrine of forgiveness, used in a balanced and responsible manner, can prove a direct highway that leads to Him.

11
THE POWER OF SUGGESTION

SUGGESTION is one of the most intriguing factors of the mind. Part of its appeal is in its mysteriousness. It operates in that mind-body fringe area about which there is little scientific understanding and a lot of pseudo-science. Here we do not need to discuss the various philosophic and psychological theories put forward to explain the phenomenon. We are interested only in the effect.

The power of suggestion appears to be almost unlimited in its capability. Indeed, it can quite readily cause death. Some Australian aborigine tribes actually use it as a method of execution. They have a sacred bone which is pointed at the offender who then quickly sickens and dies.

No degree of education or of sophistication is sufficient to guarantee immunity. I didn't think I could be tricked myself, but I was, some years back when I was a graduate student at a university. An optician told me I needed glasses which I couldn't afford. Almost immediately I developed headaches which I attributed to eyestrain. But later, after a specialist assured me the optician was mistaken, the headaches quickly disappeared.

Many of us have had the experience of feeling quite well until two or three people told us we looked tired and sick. Then our feeling of well-being started to deteriorate.

Hypnosis is an extreme case of suggestion. Under hypnotic sleep a person can have a suggestion so imbedded into his mind that he will subsequently carry it out and even attempt to rationalize his action. Thus if the subject is told while under hynosis to put out a light later, he may not remember the instruction when he comes around, but he will switch off the light. If asked why, he may say that the light was hurting his eyes or that he thought the circuit was going to blow, etc., and really believe it.

Salesmanship depends a great deal on suggestion, as we know to our sorrow when we buy a vacuum cleaner that we don't really need. After the salesman has gone we wonder what got into us to do such a thing.

Ideas are extremely suggestive. The speech of the politician, the pitch of the door-to-door sect evangelist, the persuasion of a book, can seem terribly convincing before we even weigh the evidence. We may find ourselves *wanting* to believe it and even being annoyed at contrary evidence.

The confidence men and the "bunco" artists use suggestion as their stock-in-trade. They can succeed in making people believe the most incredible things. Think of the times that the Brooklyn Bridge has been sold! Reportedly, one scoundrel actually cashed a check made out against the Left Bank of the Mississippi!

Impostors rake out fortunes by making people believe they are God or the Messiah, or that they have a copyrighted pipeline to God, or a blueprint for the future.

Possibly the saddest area where suggestion is abused is in some faith healing. The fact that many physical complaints either have a psychological basis or are influenced by psychological factors supplies the grain of truth upon which suggestion can feed. Since pain symptoms are often quite susceptible to removal by suggestion, it is not hard to give an illusion of healing. This has always been a multi-million-dollar racket. (Of course, this is not true of all faith healing by any means.)

The effectiveness of suggestion is dependent on the emotional atmosphere. While we are not "turned on," our critical powers seem sufficiently able to protect us; but emotion appears to neutralize logic and predispose toward belief. With the demagogue, the rabble-rouser and the "hot-gospeler," the stirring up of emotion is naked and unashamed, but with the door-to-door salesman it is much more subtle. He quietly arouses in us an emotional concern for the safety, welfare, and well-being of ourselves and our families. We are then mentally set in favor of his suggestions.

From all this it begins to look as if suggestion is a pernicious evil to be avoided at all costs. This is not so at all. In fact, we owe a great deal to it. It was suggestion that helped to persuade us to be good citizens instead of delinquents, to be educated instead of dropouts, to enter friendships instead of being lonesome, etc. Look behind most of our achievements and we will see that they are fruits of helpful suggestion given somewhere.

Suggestion is only bad when it dishonors the critical faculties of the personality. When someone does this to us it is an affront to our dignity. When we allow it to happen we are degrading our creation in the image of God.

Suggestion is a valuable imaginative element that stimulates discovery. It gives us the hunch that something is there long before we come to it. To accept the hunch uncritically is irresponsible and leads to error, but to take it as a hypothesis to be examined and tested is the way to truth. Science operates on the suggestions which may come from circumstances, events or people. Newton started investigating the idea of gravitation after the apple fell on his head. The planet Pluto was discovered because the theoreticians said it had to be there.

The ethical way to use suggestion in selling an idea is first to make sure we are convinced ourselves, and, if not, to appraise our degree of certainty. Our presentation should never exceed that level. We should use only such emotional factors as are sufficient to create rapport and never use emotional pressure to circumvent critical appraisal. Finally, we should deliberately encourage the subject to think the thing through himself.

If this is the proper approach, it may be asked: Why use suggestion at all? Why not just state the facts and leave it at that? Actually this completely unpressured, unemotional approach is impossible if we really care about what we are putting over. Whenever there is concern, there will be a powerful element of suggestion.

But even if this were possible it would be undesirable. It would be throwing away a powerful element in promotion of a multitude of things that are essential or desirable for human welfare. You don't outlaw the use of gelignite just because of its obvious dangers.

Where does this leave us as far as our task of evangelism is concerned? One thing is obvious: we can no longer be so irresponsible as to use the heavy emotionalism of the past, the screaming histrionics, and the tear-jerking deathbed stories. Neither can we be so unethical as to deliberately create a hypnotic tension to gain our ends.

Actually, many preachers do use a kind of hypnosis without knowing it, especially in the "appeal" or "altar call." The endless sequence of verses of the decision hymn, punctuated by intoned repetition of such calls as "Come to Jesus, come to Jesus," the loud prayer monotone—all this is hypnotic suggestion. Prolonged appeals may have the same effect by inducing mental fatigue which is a condition for hypnosis.

However, the "take it or leave it" offhand attitude will not do either. The man in the congregation must know that any decision that is made has to be his own, but he must also be made aware that it is of the utmost urgency.

The preacher's own involvement is a powerful factor in the right kind of suggestion. This was very noticeable in the

THE POWER OF SUGGESTION

New Testament preachers. Even now, when they are at the enormous disadvantage of not being with us in person, their words have a compelling power. The personal involvement generates the enthusiasm which quickly gets to us. We know how hard it is to turn down a really enthusiastic but humble salesman. The suggestion to accept is most powerful.

The use of authority is also decisive. Billy Graham's preaching features this constantly. His points are backed by statements like, "The Bible says," or "God says." Even in negative references where he is knocking undesirable things, he quotes from prominent men who are well known as authorities in their fields.

Billy Graham does this responsibly but some do not. It is only too easy to support one's views by verses of Scripture taken out of context or by putting them into the mouths of the great. Fortunately this is increasingly becoming more difficult because people are more educated now. There was a time when nobody knew any better so preachers could get away with literary murder.

The testimony of the preacher's own experience has a most telling effect, hence the New Testament appeal to *be* witnesses (Ac 1:8). People are suspicious of theory or of second-hand references. They want the truth straight from the horses's mouth. When a man relates what has happened to *him,* we are compelled to listen.

A deliberate and emphatic manner of address, but without shouting or pseudo-drama, also has its effect. When point after point, all dead center, are punched home, the impact grows. This includes the repetitive element too, so noticeable in the methods of Jesus, and typically Oriental. If the message consists of one central idea rammed home in several ways, not only will it be easily remembered, but it will effect its own cumulative suggestion upon the will.

But the power of suggestion is relevant to much more than messages. There is a crowd effect too, possibly related to the "belongingness" instinct referred to earlier. Whatever the crowd does and says seems to compel us to do the same. This is the reason for the fear that parents have (and justifiably so) when their children get into bad company.

It works the other way too. When a person comes into association with a group of vital Christians there is always a powerful suggestion to him to accept what they accept. With young people the effect is particularly marked.

Finally, it ought to be added that attitudes carry suggestive power. A Christian who not only believes in God but acts like it, will be a telling witness. If, however, he acts just like a nonbeliever, the results will be tragic. For if he panics when things go wrong, or racks his personality with the torture of anxiety, he is acting as if God does not exist. On the other hand, if it is obvious that he is expecting God to take care of him and maintains a calm confidence in all his troubles, his belief in God will be evident. Since these attitudes are automatic indications of what a man really believes rather than what he merely says, the suggestion will be quite penetrating.

12
EXPERIMENTAL RESULTS

PSYCHOLOGICAL KNOWLEDGE is obtained in two ways: generalized experience and controlled experiment. In generalized experience the whole of living becomes the laboratory. The psychologist observes people in action and picks up patterns that occur time after time in apparently identical circumstances. From these he develops laws of behavior. In these circumstances there cannot be much control of the variables; therefore, the possibility of error is considerable. However, it is minimized by taking a large number of instances. The more frequently a sequence recurs in the same circumstances, the more we can be sure that there is a definite relation and no mere chance effect. Over the years a large body of reliable results has been built up in this way. Most of the psychological information used in this book has come from this source.

The method of controlled experiment is much more exacting. Here the psychological laws are generated in vigorous laboratory conditions. All variables are deliberately controlled to guarantee that the effect observed is being determined solely by the cause under study and by no other factors. The process is infinitely more difficult than in physics, but human behavior is so complex, and persons are not readily subject to experimental conditions as are things. Also, this procedure is limited to isolated sequences of behavior rather than to broad life processes. However, some most interesting facts have been determined this way.

The area that we are most concerned with as psychologists of evangelism is attitude change. Our task is to cooperate with and be the agents of the Holy Spirit in bringing about a permanent change in people from wrong attitudes toward God, others, and life itself. Experimental psychology has tested many methods of approach to attitude change, and we can learn a lot from the results, the more relevant of which are summarized below. In many cases they reinforce what has been said in earlier chapters.

Two types of attitude change must be considered: congruent and incongruent. Congruent change is change in the same direction as the existing attitude, such as in strengthening it or amplifying it. An example is when we seek to change a person's interest in Christ to a committal to Him. Incongruent change is to *reverse* a direction of attitude, such as trying to bring about a Christ-centered life from a self-centered orientation. As might be expected, the life experiments show that incongruent change is far more difficult to effect than congruent change.

In either case a great deal depends on the intensity of the existing attitude. Jewish people who suffered at the hands of nominally "Christian" Germany during the Nazi regime seldom became Christians. Neither do fanatical Muslims. Conversion never ceases to be possible, but the effort involved may have to be very great and may need to be continued over a long period of time. In these cases we are starting way behind second scratch.

Obviously the first step is to neutralize the hostility; but in attempting to do this, it is only too easy to make the situation worse. This will happen if rebuttal is tried. Thus, if we tell the Jewish people that maybe the figures are distorted, or perhaps there were two sides to the question, they will be outraged. It is better to admit and deplore these terrible crimes and point out how utterly contradictory they were to all that Jesus taught. They must be made to see that Jesus is on their side and against His unworthy pseudo-followers.

This hostility can be used, just as a sailing ship uses even adverse winds. But more than words are required to move a sustained negative attitude. As indicated in chapter 2, the unconscious has sustained an attitude that is away from Christ. This will be immovable until enough favorable elements have been introduced to provide a counterweight. The most auspicious source for this will be the impact of Christian lives that express the best in Christlike attitudes. But even this will take time to permeate those hidden recesses.

The possibility of change is related to the complexity of the resistance. If a person has only one objection, this is relatively easily overcome; but if he has many, the cumulative effect will be greater than the sum of each one taken separately. Objections tend to reinforce one another. Thus if a contact's only objection to accepting Christ is his unwillingness to give up a bad habit, changing him will not be difficult. But if, in addition, his family objects, if he is critical of the church, if he has been hurt by a Christian, and he has intellectual objections as well, his resistance may be almost invulnerable.

However, it is possible that this complexity may be more apparent than real. Perhaps it is merely a cover-up for one basic problem: an *unwillingness* to believe. In this case, when that is overcome, all the objections evaporate together.

But if the person is honestly seeking, the number of his objections *will* have a cumulative effect. Any hypothesis can have one or two objections without much hurt; but, as these mount, the probability that the hypothesis is true rapidly diminishes.

Once again, it is not wise to meet the objections head on. That generally leads to a mere merry-go-round of words. The best plan is to try to show that the problems raised are irrelevant to the main issue anyway, which they usually are. Focus on Christ and emphasize the challenge of commitment.

Dislodging objections also depends on their relatedness, whether they are considered with one another. If a man has two objections, for instance, that he is bothered by an apparent contradiction in the Bible and he doesn't like baptism, each one can be dealt with separately and the problem may be relatively mild. But if he has a whole string of intellectual difficulties, they will reinforce one another.

This strength is due in such a case to an implicit underlying suggestion, usually that Christianity is invalid or intellectually untenable. This factor delivers the negative punch.

The problem is that logic appears more devastating than it really is. Of course, if the logic is watertight, nothing can be done about it. But it seldom is. There are usually factors inadvertently left out. In any case, life has a habit of being beyond logic. Most people will readily agree to this, opening the door for a shift to experiential grounds, which constitutes a much more favorable battlefied. Most agnostics and atheists are won in this area, and almost never in the intellectual arena.

Resistance based on a combination of related factors is significantly increased if there is any emotional content. This is particularly noticeable with Jewish people. To become Christians they must run counter to racial loyalty, family obligation, national reaction to "Christian" persecution against Jews, etc. The barriers become formidable.

When such emotion is present, handling the situation is particularly difficult because the discussion can quickly become personal. Loyalty or prejudice are ready springboards for a fight any day. But somehow the emotion has to be diffused.

If loyalty is the problem, it has to be shown that the Christian commitment is in the best interests of family, race, or nation *in the long run*. If we can succeed in doing this, the emotion will work on our side. This is not trickery by any means. If Christianity is true at all, it is God's best plan in every situation.

It has been shown that resistance to attitude change is proportional to the strength of needs served by the existing attitude. Thus, if a person is insecure and unsatisfied egowise, he may take pride in his intellectual objections to Christianity and they may, therefore, be fulfilling his inner need. If so, he will be most reluctant to let them go, no matter how convincing the rebuttals. It is of the greatest importance, therefore, to look behind the objections for the real target to attack.

Contrary to what is believed by many, experiments show that the unintelligent or uneducated person is harder to reach than his more cultured counterpart. Maybe it is because he is aware of his limitations and feels at a disadvantage, so, for safety's sake, he feels he must resist any attempt to change him. It may also be that there is less point of contact. Christianity has a strong intellectual cast, and most evangelistic messages are theologically colored. The uneducated person has little background to appreciate this, whereas the educated man has. This shows, incidentally, that the education programs of missionaries have strong psychological justification.

Billy Graham says that he has the same message for Pennsylvania coal miners as he does for the Oxford dons. This is certainly true in that he calls for repentance, faith, and committal to Christ in both cases. Nevertheless, he slants the message somewhat when educated men are present. He may refer to French existentialists, some abstruse scientific theory, or a development in literature. It is only for a moment, but it is sufficient to make contact with the intelligentsia without alienating the others.

It is a bad mistake to talk down to less highly educated

people. The "let me make it very simple for you" approach is patronizing and insulting to their dignity. Furthermore, many of these people are highly intelligent. If they receive the impression that the evangelist thinks he is superior, all contact is lost.

Neither do the truths presented have to be less profound. Whatever our audience, it deserves our best and not a watered-down substitute. But it must be presented to intellectuals with the jargon of academic circles. It must be translated in terms of their environment with illustrations that suit their interests.

It is equally disastrous to pretend to be highbrow in dealing with intellectuals. After all, their academic interests are only one part of their life. Generally they are just like everyone else, majoring almost entirely on the business of living. That is the plane where they need to meet Christ. Otherwise they may assume that religion is some kind of intellectual game that we want to play with them.

A good deal of study has been carried out to determine whether people possess a general persuadability trait. Evidence thus far suggests that there is such a factor, but that it is not particularly potent. However, it has been shown that generaly females are more persuadable than males, obviously a well-known fact to the door-to-door salesman! But males with feelings of personal inadequacy are more persuadable than females similarly troubled.

This difference is probably due to the greater degree of aggressiveness in men. Nowadays they are not as prone to mix it with fists but they do love a fight with words and ideas for ego superiority. Since the gospel is usually presented by another person there is always a natural setting for an ego fight which starts with rejection of the new idea. This general problem has been dealt with in chapter 4. The implication of this greater resistance in men is that the evangelist must be much more careful of ego problems when making the presentation to them than he is to women.

Man's other detected difference of lower resistance where there are feelings of inadequacy is probably due to the heightened consciousness of need. The man feels he is unable to cope, but desperately needs to do so. He is the drowning man clutching at a straw. The Christian gospel offers him power to be the man he wants to be, and thus has tremendous appeal. Since there are inevitably quite a number of these sufferers in any audience, it pays to emphasize this transforming effect of the gospel.

The relevance to the counseling situation is obvious. Most of those who come to us for this help have feelings of inadequacy or they would not be there. Of course, the counselor has an ethical responsibility to deal with the problem they have come to ask about, but this is usually not an isolated thing, but a symptom of a more general personality disorder. This makes the Christian message of the utmost relevance, and provides a ready-made opportunity to present it.

Actual tests have also shown that a person's openness to an attempt to change his attitudes depends a great deal on whether the group he belongs to favors that change. But this is only potent when his membership or acceptance in the group really *matters* to him.

Thus if a boy is a member of a gang which is hostile to religion, and he really needs that gang and its approval, he is going to be extremely hard to win or change in any way. This is why parents of young delinquents are often advised to move to another city. Without the inertia from the group, a delinquent is going to be much easier to rehabilitate.

Some slum workers, because of this factor, avoid the individual approach altogether, and attempt to win the gang as a whole. The gang is progressively involved in a mission or social program until the whole group has a stake in the Christian message. Primitive tribes are often won first as tribes for this very same reason.

The first natural reaction of the evangelist who sees his efforts stymied by a group is to lash out at the group. This is terrible strategy because then the contact, out of loyalty, has to defend his group. Parents often make this mistake. Actually, loyalty to the group can be used beneficially. The individual contact can be made to see that his becoming a Christian may be an effective way in which he can contribute to their welfare.

In view of the well-known practices of demagogues, some research has been done on the role of crowds in attitude-changing. It has been found that if a person is part of a crowd (e.g., a meeting) which is favorable to the attitude desired, then participation in the crowd predisposes that way. But if the crowd is unfavorable, the impact will tend to block the change.

Crowds seem to exercise a kind of hypnotic effect. A person who on his own would never dream of violence may commit the most atrocious crimes when part of a mob. Similarly, a man may be in an evangelistic meeting and be totally unmoved by the message, yet may feel impelled to join those making decisions if a number go forward.

The psychology of this feature is the same as that described in chapter 6. Fortunately, or unfortunately, the effect is quite transitory and evaporates when the crowd disperses. The rioter becomes a law-abiding citizen once more and the convert slips back into the world.

The only way that crowd psychology can be utilized in Christian evangelism is to give continuity to the crowd effect. Thus the rousing youth rally must have its extension and counterpart in the youth groups in the local church so that the convert is made to feel that he still belongs to it.

Perhaps the greatest value of the crowd for our purposes

is the "trigger effect." We may promote the Christian cause among our contacts in the local situation but never seem to get them over the edge to make that critical committal. When this groundwork has been well done, the effect is usually permanent.

A lot has been said and written about the advantages and disadvantages of the "appeal" for public commitment where the convert is asked to signify his decision by coming to the front of the building, kneeling at a penitent form, or verbally making a confession (profession) of Christ. Just how old these practices are is difficult to tell, but certainly baptism has always been a means of indicating public committal. The research results bear out the wisdom of decisions being made public. When this occurs, the attitude change is more stable and permanent.

The reasons for this are rather obvious. The requirement for public confession makes decision-making more difficult. Anyone can make a decision in his own mind because he has no bridges to burn behind him. But he has to be much more serious to overcome his shyness and have the courage to make his decision public. Also, the public decision tends to make his decision permanent because of the loss of face if he should renege on it. It is noteworthy that Paul called for such confession (Ro 10:9-10).

Recently there has been increasing demand for audience participation in the proclaiming of the message by replacing of monologue (the sermon) with dialogue or group discussion. Some experimental work has been carried out on the relative effectiveness of the lecture versus group discussion.

The method of attempting to change attitudes by lecturing or sermonizing has not fared well when put to the acid test of experiment, but the group-discussion method has. This means that the most effective method of evangelism would be to involve the contact in an evangelistic discussion in a group in which the message is brought out from them by skillful leadership. The big factor here is undoubtedly ego satisfaction. We do not like having things imposed on us because this suggests submission to another person. In the discussion method, the suggestion for change appears to be coming from ourselves and therefore is much more acceptable.

In view of these results, it certainly seems to be in order to use group discussion more in evangelistic work. But it should be kept in mind that this is much more difficult to use effectively. In the sermon or monologue the factors are largely in the control of one man. In the group discussion many people are participating, and no one can predict what they will say or do. Thus it is harder to control the situation. A great deal depends on the skill and force of the group leader in keeping the discussion on the rails. It also calls for careful preparation, especially of the questions to be raised. This kind of group discussion is not free discussion nor open conversation. It is the use of group ideas to spotlight the message of the gospel. If the talk just wanders, it will be pointless for evangelistic purposes.

Also, unless great care is taken, group discussion may lose the sense that God is speaking. In the sermon, God is speaking to people through the man. They can't talk back to the speaker, so they are forced to talk back to God, which is the ideal result. In the discussion they are talking back to one another. This doesn't exclude the possibility that they are, at the same time, meeting a challenge from God, but few people realize this.

When the challenge is coming from without, as in preaching or personal dealing, it has been shown that the resistance to the message will be proportional to the extent in which the proponent is considered to be an outsider. Paul apparently had this in mind when he wrote, "And unto the Jews I became as a Jew, that I might gain the Jews" (1 Co 9:20-23).

There are many applications of this principle. It suggests that the most influential minister will be the man who is well

EXPERIMENTAL RESULTS 115

accepted as a part of his community. It means that social fellowship with people is vitally important. It favors the doctor-to-doctor, teacher-to-teacher, youth-to-youth, Rotary-to-Rotary approach in personal evangelism.

In general, experimental results so far have not been startling. Mostly they bear out what we would expect from common-sense considerations. This science is only in its beginnings. With more research, we may be able to eliminate much of the hit-and-miss approach about the human side of evangelism.

13
MASS MEDIA

MASS MEDIA in aspect to evangelism warrants separate treatment because many of the foregoing results do not apply.

The advance of mass communications in our time has been one of the most exciting developments in an age when science is continually capturing the headlines. Before long, strategically placed satellites in the sky will enable one man to be heard and seen by the whole world. Apparently not even language will be a barrier because of electronic translation equipment.

Possibilities for evangelism seem unlimited. If "evangelize" means to "preach" then we may indeed be able to evangelize the world. Billy Graham has already achieved enormous TV coverage of his meetings, especially in England. But since the cost of such television coverage is well nigh astronomical, it becomes a matter of great importance to determine how effective this means is, or is likely to be.

It is important to note that, *in any type of program,* television's effectiveness is a two-edged sword, for if it is effective for the good it will also be effective for the bad. If the electronic eye can persuade people to change their lives toward God it can also convince them to change their lives toward Satan. The more effective it proves to be, the more we shall all be at the mercy of those who can afford to use television for their purposes.

Gloomy generalizations have already been made. Because

crime has increased since World War II, and TV has steadily and increasingly been used by the multitude, it has been claimed that this crime is due to the violence portrayed in the programs that viewers watch. But crime is increasing everywhere, even in places where there is no television. So many variables are affecting social change that it is more likely that television is being affected by these factors rather than vice versa.

One thing is beyond doubt: mass media is having a great effect on people's knowledge. The whole world is quickly becoming an open book to everybody, and this in an entertaining form.

Thus far, controlled experiments on the effect of television have seemed to indicate that the programs tend to change people's attitudes on relatively unimportant things, but not on issues which are really important to them. Thus, a popular program that advocates a change in cosmetics may sell out all supplies of the promoted product almost overnight, but the same program pitching for safer driving will hardly dent the casualty statistics.

The reason is not hard to see. Changing from one lipstick to another makes no demand upon the personality and may, in fact, appeal to cupidity or vanity, but the other change calls for a revolution in personal attitudes and, at the same time, it hits at ego confidence. It takes far more than a simple program to bring about that kind of result.

Actually, it looks as if television has little power in getting people to change their vote, let alone their lives. People become more knowledgeable about the candidates as a result of a program but apparently it takes other factors to make them change from one candidate to another.

At this stage all the evidence points to the assessment that the effect of TV on people's attitudes is superficial. Perhaps the sheer volume of the programming is a factor. We are so bombarded by messages and influences seeking to change us in one direction or another that we could end up as personality chameleons. Apparently we just get case-hardened to it all and dismiss from the mind most of the appeals even before the next program starts.

This is borne out by studies comparing the effect of the mass media and personal persuasion. The man-to-man approach is definitely more effective when attitude changes are involved. Of course, the mass media may well prove to have a cumulative effect in time. Whereas one shot may not move us, a steady bombardment could be quite a different matter.

In any case, it is evident that our hopes that television and radio will provide a shortcut to winning the world for Christ are fruitless. It is beginning to look more and more as if God has ordained that He wants this to be done largely on a person-to-person basis.

Many churches are now broadcasting their services and there are reports of remarkable conversions, but these are comparatively rare. The massive Billy Graham telecasts have brought many decisions and if these are harvested into permanent Christian associations this will be fine. But it is to be expected that the losses here will be even greater than those for mass meetings.

Use of mass media for evangelism must be considered over against the other methods, especially in view of the enormous difference in costs. For the same cost as a $400 weekly telecast, a church could employ two more ministers in the United States and three times as many in lands like Australia. Since the personal approach is so much more effective, the television method would appear to be extremely poor economy.

In the case of the Graham saturation broadcasts, the situation is somewhat different. It is true that if the money spent on these programs were put into personnel, ministers and missionaries could be supported for years. But the catch is, the money would not be available for this. People will give for something as glamorous as a national broadcast but not for unexciting run-of-the-mill evangelism. Granted, this is wrong, but that's the way things are.

One of the reasons for the relative ineffectiveness of religious broadcasting is that much of it uses the direct pitch or sermonic approach and is incredibly dull. Who, in his right mind, wants to listen to or view an hour-long commercial?

A message has always a better chance of getting over if it is camouflaged in a situation so interesting that the viewer can identify with it. Plays, films, and life stories do this much more effectively than the sermon. The trouble is, for this to be done well, the cost goes up even higher.

Perhaps we have made a mistake in assuming that television is an evangelistic method whereas its right place is a *prelude* to evangelism, a John the Baptist which prepares the way and then hands the job over to the personal witness. This function would be that described in chapter 9 on background rapport. This also would be similar to the way the politicians use the medium. They know it is not going to get them elected, but they also know that it can create such a favorable atmosphere for them that personal persuasion becomes easier.

The telecasting of worship services does not help much in creating a pleasant image. In fact, it often proclaims to the whole world just how dull and anachronistic much of our worship has become.

News is a far better approach. Many heartwarming and heart-moving things are happening in our Christian communities which the public never knows about. News stories of these events ought to be garnered and told through the mass media. This will *show* Christianity in action and will be far more convincing than mere talk. And this kind of presentation is free!

If we don't have this kind of news, let's go out and make some. News is generated when the love of God meets human need. It is our job to bring the two together.

All that has been said here should not detract from the

value of the great missionary broadcasting organizations that have been such a breakthrough on new missionary methods since World War II. They have succeeded in giving the gospel message a coverage which was not even remotely possible by normal methods.

They may assume an even greater importance in the years to come, especialy in Asia where nationalist influences are steadily driving out the resident missionaries. It may well be that for many years to come the airwaves will be the only vehicle for the message in such lands as India and China. The percentage of converts from the total number of listeners can never be expected to be very large, but these would not have been won at all without broadcasting.

The most effective outreach will be in those countries where the sowing of the seed over the air can be followed by those who water and tend the seed on the ground. Maybe a whole new missionary strategy will arise combining the spiritual air force and the spiritual army. The bombardment from the air will loosen up the enemy strongholds, enabling the ground forces to go in for personal contact.

But, initially, the conquest of the heart will always be more difficult than any military campaign. In times of revival, people may appear to respond en masse, but that can only be the sum of numerous *individual* conversions.

Perhaps one last question on mass media should be asked. To what extent does the broadcasting audience act as a group and therefore come under some of the psychological findings on a group referred to earlier?

Apparently very little. A group is more than a number of individuals. To be a true group psychologically the member of the group must be conscious of a relationship which somehow binds him together with the others. This may be a common purpose or a common interest. The binding element may be very superficial indeed, such as all listening to the same speaker or even all watching the same thing.

Mass Media

The broadcast audience seldom has this unity. They may be all listening to the one program, but unless they can see each other or sense each other, they are not likely to function as a group.

However, sometimes a broadcaster *can* succeed in creating at least an illusion of this, for both mass hypnosis and mass hysteria have happened on occasion. But this is always an artificially induced situation.

This chapter has been a discouraging one, but it is best for us to face the facts. We ought to have guessed it anyway. In evangelism as well as anywhere else, we are called to take up the cross. That means personal involvement, and electronics can never replace that necessity.

Whether a pastor should use paid radio or TV may well be a matter of money. If there are surplus funds available after the regular program has been provided for, then the media may provide needed public relations, and may even win a soul or two. But if money is scarce, it doesn't appear that it makes for good economy. The story is very different for free services; these should be availed of at every opportunity.

14
THE PERSONAL ANGLE

AT THE CLOSE of this study on the psychology of evangelism, it is necessary to pay some attention to an important fact referred to earlier. Psychological principles apply to the average person in average circumstances and therefore may not apply in a particular case or at a particular time.

This means that the task of the evangelist who is using the psychology of religion is not finished when he has applied all the scientific knowledge available. This can seldom get further than generalities, whereas the secret of impact is in specificness.

Each contact must be studied as a separate case and each application of psychological principles must be unique to that instance. Psychology is not a rule-of-thumb system to be used willy-nilly. There is nothing mechanical about human nature. Psychology provides the background understanding out of which the evangelist can frame his approach, provided he knows enough about his contact.

This is why personal evangelism is necessarily slow. My own experience has been that it takes anywhere from six months to two years before a significant decision can be expected. Not all of this time is required to gain the necessary understanding of the person. Much of it will be necessary for the development of rapport and belongingness as described in previous chapters.

Just buttonholing a stranger, witnessing to him and pressing for a decision will likely do more harm than good. Most responsible people react negatively and often quite violently to this kind of assault. It shows a fundamental lack of respect for human dignity and personality. The stranger approached is more of a statistic than a person. A man only becomes a person to us when we become aware of his individuality: that which makes him who he is and nobody else. A contact becomes a person when we can call him by name and when his name represents something unique and meaningful to us.

Even in audience or mass evangelism, this personal element has to be involved if the decision is going to mean anything. Of course, as a man in the crowd the convert is anonymous; but when he responds, he has to be dealt with on a personal basis. This is basic procedure either in the inquiry room or in subsequent follow-up.

Since the evangelistic approach is basically a decision to enter another person's life, it cannot be entered into lightly or casually. It is personality surgery and therefore requires the utmost care and sense of responsibility.

Neither can the process be impersonal from the evangelist's side. He cannot keep his own life and personality completely private. It is not like teaching mathematics, for example, where the teacher is merely passing on information which requires no personality change. The evangelist must pass on something of himself when he presents the message.

Conversion is the product of a personality merger; in other words, a friendship. The friendship does not have to be of the eternal kind, neither does it have to be one of deep emotional involvement. These are reserved for those few friends which we need for our own meaningful existence. But there does have to be self-giving in which the contact is given a glimpse of our own heart.

The friendship between the soul winner and the convert may not be one that will require a great deal of subsequent social contact, but it will mean the setting up of bonds that will last long after the decision to follow Christ has been made.

To be honest, we must want the person for his own sake and not just because we want another convert. The friendship must not merely be a means to an end. "Using" friendship like that is most undesirable.

To be true to our integrity we must really have a love for people for *themselves*. Then evangelism becomes a by-product of self-giving love and not the reason for it. We want our friend to have the very best and that means Christ.

Our sincerity on this point is tested by our reaction after their conversion. If we just drop them, then it means we had very little personal interest in them in the first place. If the love was real, then we would be just as interested in continuing with them afterward as before.

In any case, the giving is not as one-sided as we might think. Evangelism is a need for the Christian personality which will wither unless it has outreach. Christ within us is hungering to reach others through us; therefore, there can be no inner peace without this kind of self-giving.

Whenever another person allows us to enter into the fellowship experience with him that supports evangelism he is making a significant contribution to our lives. The realization of this truth will effectively keep us from the pride and pharisaism in which we might consider ourselves as spiritually "slumming." We are not self-sacrificingly stretching out a good-Samaritan hand to the poor soul in the swamp. We are in there with him, but with a difference. Our other hand is in the hand of God.

It is this love, this mutualness of need, that will make us study our new friend. But this analysis will not be the type that the psychologist makes. Our friend cannot now be a patient under the scrutiny of ourselves as pseudo-psychiatrists. We should not be looking for hidden complexes or incipient pyschotic tendencies. Rather, we must treat him as a normal human being, neither any better nor worse than we are psychologicaly, or in any other way for that matter.

Instead, the love of Christian concern will recognize that he has basic needs, especially the central drive to find fulfillment in a satisfying relation with others, which, of course, is true for us too. As we get to know him we will come to understand his particular heartaches and frustrations. As he comes to know that he is not alone in this, and that we have our problems too, but that with us they are in process of solution, his spirit will be buoyed up and he will reach out toward God for help too.

Apparently the wisdom of how we present the message is quite secondary to person-to-person rapport. The merging of personalities in love and friendship is the important factor, for in that way the Christ within us confronts the other person's heart too.

This does not mean that the presentation of the message cannot help. It can, especially if it is tailored to meet the personality needs. But just to recite scripture texts or explain theological systems is of little value. This is little better than the parroted spiels of the door-to-door sectarians. Jesus did not bombard the woman at the well with clichés. He found her need and sought to minister to it. What He said to Nicodemus and the rich young ruler was different again, because their needs were different. He had no canned evangelism.

Whenever possible, the witness approach is best. If our contact's needs are similar to experiences we have been through or are going through, we can tell just how Christ and His message have helped us. If the need is radically different, perhaps we know how the gospel has helped someone else with a similar problem.

Knowing him well will enable us to be specific in our application. For example, it will save us from missing him by talking about how Christ releases from the agony of guilt if he is not particularly afflicted that way. It will enable us to show him how union with Christ gives eternal life when he is lonely for a loved one who has recently died. It will also keep us from the tragic faux pas which can easily occur when he has tragedy in his life that we do not know about.

At first glance, the need for this kind of skill and insight is frightening. But it need not be. We needn't dash off for technical training in counseling. Much of it is tact, which is another word for loving concern, the ability to get into the other person's skin until we can feel what he feels.

Sermon evangelism cannot have this intimacy. Perhaps we get closest to it when the minister has been in a parish long enough to immerse himself in its life and heart. Then when he prepares his messages he can have his people in mind. Phillips Brooks once said that he got most of his messages from his pastoral visitation. The needs would stimulate his mind to find how the gospel could minister to them. Many effective ministers have used their counseling sessions as a basis for heart-moving books and sermons.

The visiting evangelist will always be at a disadvantage. Except in the most general terms, he cannot know exactly where to aim emotionally. Billy Graham attempts to overcome this by getting his staff to do research beforehand in the area where the mission is to be held. Reggie Thomas does much more. He spends hours during the crusade visiting in the homes of those who have shown interest. But none of this can begin to approach the effectiveness of the person-to-person cultivation over a long period of time.

Thus there will be no computer age for evangelism; no automation will put the personal worker out of work. Psychology will help us to understand ourselves better, but there will always be a gap which can be bridged only by the tender, loving outreach of the human spirit.